SAMANTHA BENNINGTON

Around the Way Publishing
Woodland Hills, California, USA

Published by
Around the Way Publishing
21700 Oxnard Sreet, Suite 660
Woodland Hills, CA 91367
AroundtheWayPublishing.com

The Library of Congress Cataloging-in-Publication Data Applied For

Samantha Bennington—
Falling Love Notes: Memories of a Rock Star Wife

p.   cm
ISBN 978-1-7355299-0-5
1. Autobiobraphy   2. Nonfiction   3. Celebrity   I. Title
2020

Printed in the United States of America

3 5 7 9 10 8 6 4 2

For interviews or information regarding special discounts for bulk purchases,
please contact us at inquiries@ATWPublishing.com

Cover Notes

The red spider lilies depicted on the cover are bright, summer flowers and are native throughout Asia. They are associated with final goodbyes, and legend has it that these flowers grow wherever people part ways for good. In old Buddhist writings, the red spider lily is said to guide the dead through samsara, the cycle of rebirth.

Cover art by Draven Bennington

Dedication

To my most important human in my life, my son Draven Bennington. You give me so much purpose in life, and I love you with all my heart.

GOLDENVOICE

BACK FROM their Wonderful
tour! A VALENTINE EXTRAVAGANZA

CIRCLE JERKS
GANG GREEN
from Boston
BAD (NOT GOOD) RELIGION
INSOLENTS

FRI.
EB. 14th

FENDERS
521 EAST 1st St.
LONG BEACH

INFO:
213-435-2838

WISH
I HAD
A DATE

ticket Master
tickets: →
ZED Long Beach / PEER Cypress, fountain Valley / Record Shack Gash For Chaos Laguna / Discount Costa M
LONDON EXCHANGE Costa Mesa / RHINO West-Wood / POP CULTURE Laguna Hills / ReBall Slut + VINYL Fetish Hu

Riddle Me This, Riddle Me That

Riddle me this, riddle me that
I am not Dr. Suess or the Cat in the Hat.

We are the same as we like to rhyme,
However, I do not Believe in time.

People come and people go
But does anyone really know?

There is a story I'm about to tell,
Do you believe in heaven or hell?

We all experience the past, present, and future,
But truth be told we need to learn to nurture.

Open your heart and open your mind,
All of us are the same kind.

Created and linked to all the same energy,
So why can't we think beyond just you and me?

Everything we do leads to me and you,
This story that I tell somewhere inside, you know it's true.

So please believe in when you are kind,
You are sharing with the world in mind.

With every action of love you do,
It always comes back and again this is true.

Some say it's Karma and I like this a lot,
And again the Universe has a plot.

A ripple affect that we all feel,
So let's bond together and begin to heal.

I lead my life on a foundation of love
and I know sometimes we all need a hug.

No one is perfect and judgement has no place,
So when we realize that, judgment has a new face.

The awakening has begun and a new song is sung.

The air, wind, sea, and trees, all include you and me.

Can you see that we are connected?

When you reflected, on this poem I wrote especially for you and the reason is because I love you!

—Samantha Bennington

Inspired by Dr. Suess, my favorite writer and poet, written in five minutes in bed because I couldn't sleep. I'm on my way to a journey of enlightenment and I truly want to take you all with me!

Foreword

I've re-written this foreword many times now, never having done this before, and have decided to keep it short and sweet. I've known Samantha Bennington and her family since 2000, when our experiences crossed paths and we became friends—actually, family. I say family because it's what means the most to Sam. I've been blessed to be considered that by her and her family.

I wasn't in Sam's life for the early years, but I've learned this from her, since I've been around for the past eighteen years: she's one of the strongest and most caring people I know, and she gives herself fully to all she loves and cares about. Her heart is one of the biggest I've been blessed to know, and I believe you'll see this for yourself after you've finished reading this book. When adversity strikes, Sam strikes back and doesn't give up. She has true quality, and is an inspiration.

Without keeping you any longer, let me say I love you Samantha. Congrats, you've done it! You're a beautiful, strong, and loving person. Thank you for your friendship, and for considering me part of your family—and for giving me the opportunity to say it in print. Never stop being who you are.

Love,

Stephen "Stef" Carpenter
Founder and lead guitarist, Deftones

Introduction

As a mother, artist, empath, music industry executive, and life coach, I have a passion for helping people manifest their dreams. I mainly work with artists, because I grew up in the music industry: I worked one-on-one with my late ex-husband Chester Bennington so he could become the lead singer for the rock band Linkin Park. It is important to me that every human being pursues their passions so they may live their happiest life. My personal and professional background provides artists with a safety-net; we all come from the same creative space and therefore have similar ambitions to live our greatest lives.

I began to write this book eight years ago and it was initially due to be released in the fall of 2017. As you will read, unfortunate tragic events happened within our family that changed my life's direction. No matter the adversity or opportunity anyone has experienced, no person is exempt from anything life may bring. This tragedy compelled me to share many heartfelt moments, as well as some of my own hardships, and I share stories here in Falling Love Notes that many people will relate to and/or have experienced. Throughout, I chose to be raw, humble, authentic, and vulnerable. My hope is to give you a different perspective of life, to know and believe in yourself enough so that no matter what life throws at you, you can identify your own purpose. As a life coach my goal is to always help you discover the key points that will get you the results of your manifestation.

My journey in writing this book stems from my desire to connect with other people from around the world. We all share the same energy and we are all connected. Therefore, raising our frequency to its highest vibration, is in the whole planet's best interest. In writing Falling Love Notes, I bare all.

Please know that throughout my life's peaks and valleys, I have learned to act with love. Falling Love Notes is, in many ways, a love letter to myself about how to maintain and remain in my truth as a mother, friend, and business person—knowing with all my heart that I needed to share with the whole word my unique perspective. By embarking on this literary journey I have come to learn there is no greater pursuit than that of self-actualization.

It's important to me that you know that I decided to form my own publishing company to support this book, Around The Way Publishing, LLC, so I could tell my story, my way, with no restrictions.

It is my hope that as you read Falling Love Notes you will feel as if we are having a personal, one-on-one conversation; so that you can take whatever speaks to you and utilize the tools placed within this story to get you closer to a healthier, more universal and mindful platform. In sharing my memories, I believe, we can together begin a conversation that will help us evolve to live more collectively and harmoniously for the greater good.

With Love,

Samantha

Abandoned Twice

"MOMMY, MOMMY WAKE UP, I'm going to be late for school. Mom. Mom! Mommy, wake up!" In her bed, my mother started to move, pushing both arms out and upward as if she was about to do a pushup. Then her body began to shake, and somehow I knew that she was going into a seizure, although, as far as I knew, she'd never had one before. Her wide-open eyes rolled into the back of her head, and she collapsed into her bed. There was no movement or sound after that, and time stood still. Confused, and too young at age seven to understand what was going on, tears of fear streamed down my face in a constant flow. It was 1978, and I didn't know anything about 911.

The sound of the telephone ringing cut through the air like a sharp knife.

"Hello?" I said, holding back sniffles of tears. "Daddy! Something is wrong with Mommy. She won't wake up!"

My dad's instructions were crystal clear. Run to three neighboring houses to see if anyone was home to help, then come right back and answer the phone when it rang.

On a Friday morning at eight-thirty AM on the last day of school before a two-week spring break. I should not have been surprised that no one was home at any of the three houses. After I raced home in a panic to answer the phone, I cried hysterically, "Daddy, no one answered. No one is home!"

"Stay put," he said, "help is on the way."

We lived in the Pacific Palisades Highlands, which is a long canyon off Pacific Coast Highway and Sunset Boulevard, so help took time in coming. Finally, people came storming through the house in what seemed to me to be very large numbers. *Thank God,* I thought to myself, *the good guys are here.* With the paramedics came members of the fire and police departments, and two of Dad's business partners.

My father and his partners were in the fashion business as a manufacturer, and specialized in plus sizes. Dad also owned several clothing lines and named several of them after me, including Lady Samantha and Samantha O. In the middle of this huge family emergency, one of Dad's partners brought his wife and the other brought his girlfriend. I was so upset, it seemed everyone was speaking in code. I didn't understand anything anyone said.

There was so much commotion, and the noise from sirens was loud enough to damage eardrums, but everyone knew exactly what to do. The paramedics lifted my mom's naked body onto a stretcher and used her very white bed sheet to cover her up. Soon, they were ready to take her away, and everyone started to leave. First the paramedics, then the firemen and police, and finally dad's business partners along with the girlfriend and the wife. Then, in the aftermath, came the silence. I was left all alone.

The phone didn't ring, and no one came. It was so quiet in the house that I could hear my own heart beat. So, I took my ball and went outside to play. After all, that was the most logical way to pass the time, especially at the young age of seven. My friends and I loved playing handball against our garage door in our cul-de-sac. That's what we did. We played handball, rode our bikes, and played Marco Polo in the pool whenever our parents let us swim.

The day was so long. I didn't know what was going on or how serious it all was, but I knew something was very wrong with my mom. I also didn't understand why every adult there left me behind. They all forgot me, even the "good guys."

For hours, I played by myself. Time must eventually have rolled to half past three or so, because my friends came home from school and we all played outside until it started getting dark and it was time for dinner. My friends were called in by their parents, one by one, and I remember standing in the alley with my ball in my hand thinking I'd better go inside; it was night time.

I was home for a while by myself. I cannot remember exactly how long, but it was long enough—too long for a child to be left on her own. Too long, especially after finding her mom and watching her have a full blown seizure. That time for me was like a horror movie. So scary, and so much action. I didn't know who or what was coming next. I just remember thinking *everyone forgot me. How could the good guys forget me? Wasn't it part of their job to be sure kids were taken care of? What were my dad's business partners thinking, leaving me all alone? They were like uncles to me. And what about my dad? Where was he?*

Turned out my dad was in San Francisco on a business trip, but I thought due to the emergency, that he would have been home much sooner. As a child, I didn't think about plane schedules or the seven or more hours it took to drive from San Francisco to the Palisades.

The door bell rang then, and when I opened the door, Julie's dad was there. Julie and I were best friends and she lived a few houses down from us. He said my dad had called and that I would be staying with them for the next two weeks, over spring break.

I said, "Okay," and he helped me pack a few things. *This isn't so bad*, I thought for a split second. Except, where was my dad? What had happened to my mom? Why wouldn't anyone say anything? I didn't know where any of my family members were. Where were Papa and Grandma? Where was my aunt Marsha? I always went places with one of them. Did any of my family know where I was?

The morning after they took my mom away, everything moved faster than I was used to. Turned out I was going on a trip with my best friend's family of four, right then and there, and that was one more person than I was used to. Our family dynamic was three. It was just my mom, dad, and me. But now I was going on a road trip to Julie's grandparents home, which may (or may not) have been near Santa Barbara or Solvang. In any case, it was very beautiful wherever they lived. It was Easter, and they were Christian. With everything else that was going on, this was another huge bit of turmoil.

My mom and dad adopted me at birth, and they are Jewish. I had never celebrated Easter before. But in spite of everything going on around me, I had fun. Julie and I got to get all dressed up in cute dresses, and Julie's family gave me a colorful Easter basket filled with chocolate bunnies, marshmallow peeps, and even a stuffed animal bunny! This was way better than Passover.

When I arrived home from my spring break vacation, my dad, my papa, and my cousin Celine were all at the house. Celine is just shy of being a year older and was my closet friend—almost like a sister. Our home was filled with all of our family and friends. It was like I came home to a party, as my grandparents, aunts, uncles, and cousins from both sides of my family were there, as well as a number of family friends. Everyone was there eating barbecue and swimming, and the house was packed.

I went to play with my cousins and felt it was so nice to be home. However, I knew I was coming home to something bad. I could feel it in my stomach, like an avocado pit. In a way, though, I was relieved to not have to deal with it as soon as I got home, and it was good to be with people I loved and trusted.

For an endless number of days, no one would tell me what happened to my mom. All I knew was that every day my dad, my extended family, and my parents' friends were either at the house or at the hospital. That's finally where I learned where my mom was. She was in the hospital, and hospital rules were that children under a certain age were too young to be allowed to visit the ICU. I didn't know that ICU meant Intensive Care Unit. All I knew was that my mom's condition was very serious.

Looking back, I don't believe anyone knew how to handle the situation. I think my dad and grandparents just followed doctor and hospital orders. My dad was on the phone constantly. There was so much to talk about: What to do next? Will she make it? How long will she be in the hospital? My only thought was *will I ever see my mom again?*

Mom was in a coma and everyone involved, including her doctors, did not know how long she would stay like that. She had suffered a brain aneurysm (a hemorrhagic stroke), and it was touch and go. Everyone involved was unsure if she was going to make it out alive, or have any sort of recovery from the severity of the aneurysm. At this point her doctors didn't know how much damage had been caused, but I gathered that it didn't look good and her chances were slim.

Our neighbors directly next to us had a recording studio in their house, and their daughter, Mindy, was one of my friends. One day Mindy's parents came up with an idea. Since the hospital would not let me see my mom, due to her very critical condition (and because I was so young), they thought I could make a tape. In that way, I could speak to my mom.

The studio itself was beautiful, and had wood paneling. It was warm and cozy, and I felt comfortable being in there with all the control panels and buttons. There were so many knobs and switches, I didn't want to touch a thing! That was the very first time I was in a recording studio, and I was kind of scared to make the tape. I didn't know what to say.

Mindy's dad was a kind man, and he guided me. "Tell your mom hello," he said. "Tell her what's going on with you, tell her anything you want her to know." He said the words in such a calm voice that I relaxed.

There was so much I wanted to say, especially because I understood that this could possibly be the last conversation I ever had with my mom. Except rather than a conversation, the tape would be like a verbal letter or postcard. Mindy's parents were going to record my voice, record me expressing my feelings to my mom, and then play it for her in the hospital. That sounded like a nice thing to do.

But then I became scared again, and I didn't want to do it. I really didn't want this to be my last memory or experience with my mother, my last words to my mom. I really didn't want to make this tape at all. I knew Mindy's dad was very kind to do this. I knew that much. I also knew his family—and all the families in our community—felt bad for us. For my dad and me. So, I made the tape with encouragement from Mindy's dad, my dad, and anyone else who chimed in.

"Mom, hi. Mmm . . . I don't know what to say," I whispered. After some encouragement from Julie's dad, I continued. "I miss you a lot Mommy. Mmm . . . I love you . . . and I hope you can come home soon . . . I hope you feel better . . . Mmm . . . School is going good . . . I did this art project and it was a lot of fun. Please wake up soon. We all want you to come home. Okay, bye Mom . . . I love you."

♥

Several months passed and I still had not gotten to see my mom. Nor, I found later, had my mom been allowed to hear the tape I made for her. This was because her medical team didn't think it would make a difference, because she was in a coma and couldn't hear. At some point the doctors told my grandmother (Mom's mother, whom I called Bubbie) that they didn't think Mom was going to make it. They thought it was time to pull the plug on her life support.

Bubbie, naturally, became hysterical and started yelling at the nurses to play her granddaughter's tape. She insisted that her daughter hear her own daughter's message. Finally, a nurse played the tape I made for my mom, and suddenly, one of Mom's fingers on her right hand moved. After many months, this was the first sign of life. It was a miracle! My mom heard my voice, even as she lay in a coma.

Her doctors and nurses were in amazement as they rushed around checking her vitals, doing whatever they needed to do to bring her to consciousness. Later, doctors told us this was a medical breakthrough, and was how the medical field first found that coma patients could hear. Soon, Mom was moved from ICU to another floor at what is now Northridge Medical Center in Northridge, California. Finally, she became awake and stable enough to see me. I expected to see my mother as she had been, but what I saw terrified me. Her head was shaved, there were tubes coming out of her throat, and much of her body was paralyzed. She didn't look at all like my mother.

After approximately six months, my mom was released from the hospital and came home. When Mom came home, she came home to a party filled with family, friends, and loved ones. That is how my family did it. My dad's side of the family was very close, and we always got together for family birthday parties, holidays, weekend visits, and trips to Papa and Grandma's cabin at Big Bear. Big Bear is about three and a half hours from LA, and has a huge, beautiful lake. In the winter it snows, and it is the closest ski resort to Los Angeles.

My cousin Celine and I always spent a lot of time together, and I loved going to my aunt Marsha's house for the weekend. Aunt Marsha is Celine's stepmom. Celine's dad, Stoney, and my dad were best friends, and after his marriage to Celine's mom ended, Stoney married my dad's sister, Marsha.

My dad and I used to play racquetball every weekend at the YMCA. That's how we got our father and daughter time. In our family, Celine was a stepdaughter and I was adopted so, even at a young age, we both knew we weren't blood related to some of our family, so we found a natural bond.

I was told about my adoption when I was four. My dad and mom sat me down in my dad's big sitting chair and said, "You were adopted at birth and came out of another mommy's tummy." I learned then that I didn't come out of my mom's tummy because she couldn't have a baby, and they wanted me so badly that I was hand picked.

It was a much easier conversation for my adopted parents then they thought it might be, I think. I understood everything they told me and it was more than okay, especially since they made me feel very special. They also told me that my biological mother was very young and could not keep me. Again, I grasped this concept fully and was not confused or angry. I loved my bio mom for giving me to another family, and for the most part I was happy—until my mom came home.

My family life had been very normal, so I thought, until what I called "the accident." Now my entire life was changing. After my mom woke up, and before she was released from he hospital, my family and I often made trips to the hospital to visit her. I hated going there and couldn't stand the smell of sickness in the air. Now that mom was home, my happy life was gone. I hardly ever saw my dad anymore, and as a matter of fact, couldn't remember a lot of my life prior to my mom getting sick.

When Mom came home from the hospital, doctors, journalists, and photographers all came to our house to film the survival of the woman who heard her daughter's voice on a recorded tape and woke up out of a coma. What a story! They always wanted us to pose for the camera. Then whomever was writing the article on the "amazing medical breakthrough" typically asked my mom to walk to the pool and sit in a lounge chair—as if we were a normal family. Then they asked me to get into the pool and swim laps, or maybe dive into the pool, as if I was so happy to show my mom the new tricks I had learned while she was away dying in the hospital.

It wasn't easy for my mom to walk to the pool. Not at all. The aneurysm caused her to be paralyzed on the entire left side of her body. She had to re-learn the most basic of skills, such as how to hold a spoon or fork, hold a pencil and form letters, tie her shoes with one arm, get dressed, and walk. She had to re-learn how do to just about everything. She was determined to recover, but the result was my mom wasn't my mom anymore. All of the re-learning caused her to become angry and frustrated, and she and my dad found themselves in the middle of a divorce. Mom was fighting for her life, and I guess he was too, in a way. We all were just trying to survive.

With my mother barely surviving this horrifically tragic, life-changing experience, I realized the aneurysm stole not just my mom's life, it stole three lives. Through her illness, our family was ripped to shreds, and I was stuck in the middle, living with a mother who couldn't care for herself and definitely could not take care of me. From the moment Mom came home, we had strange nurses in and out of the house. This on top of my father living with his new girlfriend (and soon to be wife) and I was stuck at eight years old with no parents who were present.

My mom and dad probably had troubles before she got sick. But if they did, I didn't know about it. Secretly, I thought my dad was lucky to be able to leave and have a normal home, but I also wondered why had he adopted me only to leave me with all this craziness? Why leave us when Mom was so sick and I was so traumatized from all the chaos? It wasn't Mom's fault. She never asked to be sick.

In addition to physical problems, "the accident," changed my mom's personality. I remember sometimes looking at her and thinking how unhappy she was, and how sad the aneurysm had made her. My mom's illness took hold of her and transformed her body, the way she looked, and her mobility, and I had to ask the question: was this a way to live?

I also thought the illness had taken her mind as well. I didn't like my own mother anymore, and I no longer felt safe with her. She often screamed at the top of her lungs and cursed at me. Every time I wanted to help her she got mad and started to scream. If I didn't eat all my food she screamed at me, even in public places. She sometimes wouldn't even call me by my name. Instead, she'd call me little bitch, slut, whore, and even cunt. It was verbal and emotional abuse, and although I didn't know what it was called, I knew it was wrong. I remember thinking *Mommy should be in heaven with God and the angels, and in peace. Maybe she would be happier? Maybe we would all be happier? Maybe I would then live a normal life with my dad? Maybe . . .*

Most of all, I didn't like that my dad had left me behind to deal with this insane situation, a situation that not even adults handled well, so why leave me? I was just a kid. I didn't know what I was doing. I was stuck in a divorce with my physically handicapped mother who was also mentally ill. And, I was going back and forth to a new home to see my dad. I felt like I was living in the movie *Mommy Dearest.*

Every night I prayed to God and told him, "When I become a mommy I promise to be a good mommy. I will never scream, be cruel, and mean to my baby. I promise!"

Even though I was stuck in this awful place between both my parents, I tried to remember what my mom had been like before her accident. I can only remember pieces of the day prior to her getting sick. I don't know why I can remember in detail all the little things, including colors and scents that happened after "the accident," but do not have a single memory of my childhood with my mom before. I do not have one memory of her—do not even remember what she looked like before she got sick without looking at a photo. Except for one thing.

The only thing I remember was the day before. We were painting my bedroom pink. I had to have my room pink because isn't that what little girls dream of? In the distance, I also heard the ice cream truck coming toward our house. I remember my mom wanted a crunch bar and they didn't have any. I improvised on ice creams and came home. I remember the smallest details from the day before the tragedy, but since "the accident" happened, I have never liked the color pink.

Stepmonster

I'M NOT SURE WHOSE bright idea it was to have Celine and me sing at the wedding of my dad and his new wife, but we did, along with our other cousin, Greg, who played piano. I remember being happy that I was a part of the wedding. After all, it was my dad, but I was terrified to sing in front of all those people! I would never have had enough courage without my partner in crime and closest cousin. We sang the song, "You Light Up My Life," by Debby Boone. I think this was the bride and groom's choice. The song was the number one song of 1977 and the biggest hit of 1970s. It won a Grammy for song of the year, and an Oscar for best song.

With dad now remarried, I was on an every other weekend schedule between my parents, and went from the Highlands to Marina Del Rey, a distance of about six miles. Eventually, my dad went to court and won custody of me, so I moved in with my dad and stepmom, and we all moved to Redondo Beach, California.

Starting a new school in the middle of junior high was extremely scary, and living with my dad and a new wife was totally scary, too. But, staying with my adopted mom, well, that would have even been scarier. Her angry outbursts, many of them directed at me, had only gotten worse. In a few short years I'd experienced my mother becoming disabled, my parents divorce, a wedding, and a new house in a new town. Here I was experiencing four of the top ten most stressful life changing events at once—and I was still only twelve.

Before I moved in with my dad, I had gone to Paul Revere Junior High in Pacific Palisades. Now I went to Hillcrest Junior High in Redondo Beach. This was weird, because at my other school, I wasn't supposed to start high school until I was in the tenth grade, but in the South Bay, in Redondo Beach, the school district was different and kids started high school in the ninth grade. So, I soon found myself at Redondo Union High. I dreaded this transition, to say the least. I really had wanted to go to Palisades Charter High School, what my friends and I called Pali High. All my friends were going to go there and I didn't know if I would ever see them again. Natalie, Jennifer, Jill, Amy, Justine, and most of all, Damon. I had known all of them my entire life. I was just becoming a teen, and that was hard enough without everything else going on in my life. Little did I know that I would soon meet my best guy friend in the whole world, a person I would come to think of as my "brother from another mother." Change can be good, but I definitely didn't know that then.

Scott and I were both in the middle of major moves. He was moving in with his father, and had previously lived in Northern California with his mom, so we had some common experiences. I will never forget the first moment I laid eyes on him. He walked down the hall at school like he was some type of god. Well, at least he looked like a god in my eyes! He had a twin Mohawk, his leather jacket was studded and painted, he wore Dr. Martens, and had the longest eye lashes ever. I wondered who the guy was? He was so cute, very cool, and reminded me of my punk friends at Paul Revere.

At my old school, I had hung out with a group of guys who were in a band called Suicidal Tendencies. Even though they were a little older, I had grown up with most of them: "Cyco Miko," and several others. Those were the good old days, when I lived with my adopted mom and had very little supervision. My girlfriends and I used to take the bus to Westwood and hang at the McDonalds there. We'd tell our parents we were going shopping, to the movies, or to a girlfriend's house to sleep over (and that's exactly what we did) but we always hung out for a little while with the guys. It was comforting, because I felt like I was looked after, like I was someone's baby sister, and these guys cared about me and protected me. I was too young to really hang out, but for the short period of time they allowed me to hang around it was pretty cool.

Anyway, Scott turned out to be my first real crush. Even though he had mostly lived in Northern California, he knew many people at my new school from visiting his dad regularly. My friend Sean and his family knew Scott's family before Scott was even born. Scott's mom and dad lived across the street from Sean's parents, and they loved Sean's mom, Flora. Flora babysat Scott's older brother, Mark, before Scott was born. Scott knew Sean from birth, and knew Danny, another neighbor, since he was three years old. Scott, Sean, and Danny. All I have to say is: #punkfrombirth!

The moment we became friends, which was a week or two after my first "Scotty Sighting," we became inseparable best friends. It went from love at first sight, to best friends for life. However, I still had a major crush on him, but we were young, and nothing was going on but flirting. From the moment we became friends, I was always with Scotty.

You can imagine the look on my dad's face when I told him about this boy that I liked. Scotty, Scotty, Scotty. I was crazy over him. I was just about to be thirteen, and when my father saw my punk rock guy for the first time . . . let's just say all he kept repeating was, "This is just a faze, it's just a faze." I'm sure there was also some, "Please God, let it just be a faze" in his commentary.

My biggest problem at my new school was that the girls I encountered were mean and territorial. They didn't like me, didn't know me, and didn't like that I had a different attitude. I, however, didn't care what they thought. Girls can be cruel at any age. The boys liked me because I was the, let's face it, "new girl" and "the shiny new toy."

One day after school some girls tried to pick a fight with me. I stood up to those who surrounded me, as half the school watched. It was a terrifying experience, but in some weird way, I gained some respect because I stood my ground.

These were girls who used to call me "rich bitch from Malibu." I wish my parents *had* been rich, but being upper middle class and from the Palisades, I guess that's how rumors start. But, you should never assume, because you never know what's going on in another person's life. It's funny if you think about it. Some people thought my life was a certain way, just from what they saw me projecting on the outside. They had no idea that life for me was living in an adult nightmare. And, being a kid, I couldn't get out. I was stuck with my parents' choices and their nightmare had become mine.

I love people. I love being social. But when I was in high school, teen hormones were flying. Kids were growing in and out of their awkward stages and trying to figure life out. I thought I had it figured out when, in reality, I had so much to learn.

It didn't take too long after my move before I had a few best girlfriends, and most people lost interest in me being "the new girl." And, with Scotty, I had my best friend. No other boy could get my attention with Scotty always around.

There was one guy, Greg, whom I kept getting introduced to at school, though. After about the twelfth time of being introduced to him, I finally turned to a girlfriend and asked, "Why do you keep introducing me to this guy?" At the time I thought it was weird and annoying, especially since Mark, my boyfriend at the time, lived right around the corner from her house. Mark was eighteen and out of high school, and was a super hot surfer who drove a motorcycle. That was so much cooler to me than dating a high school boy.

The reality was, though, that I didn't really care about boyfriends then, and would always choose to hang with my girlfriends and Scotty before my boyfriend—or any other cute guy for that matter. I was always pissing off my boyfriend and canceling plans with him. I was young, my life was brand new, and I didn't care much about dating. Don't get me wrong, I loved the attention, but I also loved to dance. That was my art, my focus, my sport, just like some kids had football, basketball, or baseball. I was all about dancing and my friends.

My adopted mom ended up buying an apartment complex in Redondo Beach that was right off of Beryl Street and Prospect. She had an apartment there, and I visited her on the typical every other weekend schedule. That worked out great because it was walking distance to Scotty's house. It also was much easier for us to hang out when I was at Mom's than at my dad's. My dad lived closer to the beach on Esplanade, between Avenues C and D. Plus, my dad was very strict and I was almost never allowed to have friends over—especially if they were boys.

Most my friends lived off Beryl Street: Scotty, Sean, Danny, Christian, and a few other of our mutual friends. The list was long. Of course they all started a little punk rock clique. I didn't realize it at the time, but right across the street from my mom's new apartment complex, lived a persistent guy who never missed an opportunity to get to know me. Greg, the new guy I kept getting introduced to, was smart. Somehow and some way he started hanging out with my friends. One of Greg's friends started to date a friend of mine, and he used that opportunity to work his way into our crowd. I now knew the guy existed. That was a step in the right direction for him. I also knew his name now. Greg Wilson.

High school was not so bad. I actually really loved it. I had many friends and got along with just about everyone. I also felt safer at school and when I was with Scotty than I did at home. Everyone thought Scotty and I were brother and sister, and he protected me as if we were. We told everyone we were, and our friends who knew we were not blood didn't care. I essentially became his little sister and, not having any brothers and sisters of my own to grow up with, I often pretended I wasn't a single child. I wanted to have siblings, just as my friends had, and wondered if I had biological brothers or sisters out there somewhere.

It felt amazing to have someone love and protect me. The reason I did not feel safe at home was due to my stepmother. Sometimes I felt like I was living a *Cinderella* story where the evil stepmother was nice in front of other people and mean behind closed doors.

My "stepmonster" and I never got along, and my father was always out of town. So, needless to say, being at school was way better than being at home. My stepmonster never treated me right, and was a completely different person in front of my dad, family, her friends—and especially strangers. She cared so much what other people thought. But, she was fake and phony, and I continued to be amazed at the energy it took to keep up her charades. She was so mean to me. I could never please her, and felt more often than not that I was a modern-day Cinderella.

As I mentioned, my father traveled for business. As his "shmatta" business, his clothing business, grew, my dad and his business partners created new clothing lines and that is how he met my nemesis, the "stepmonster." She was a sales rep for another manufacturer and somewhere between New York and Los Angeles they crossed paths.

I realize that every time my stepmonster saw me, my presence reminded her that my dad had a life, a full life, before he met her. Every time she took one look at me, I got the feeling that she hated me, that I was in her way. I took up much of my dad's free time, and she wanted kids of her own. My mom being disabled meant my dad had to play both parental roles. On top of it all, I was adopted and she was having a hard time getting pregnant.

I always knew my dad loved his wife as a wife and me as his daughter. Why did I understand the dynamics and my evil stepmonster couldn't? She was a grown woman and I was thirteen. I often wondered what was wrong with this crazy lady for her to be so jealous. The love my father had for us was completely different. Besides, it's gross to be jealous over someone's child.

When my stepmonster and my dad announced they were adopting a baby boy, I hoped my home life was about to get better. The adoption was a success and suddenly I had a baby brother named Alex. He was just the cutest little butter ball and the happiest baby. Having a little brother that was adopted, as I was, was comforting to me, and I thought that would naturally bond us together.

I was so excited, and thought how awesome it was to finally get to be a big sister.

On one hand, being a big sister was going to be amazing, but let's not forget I was in high school and all I cared about was being with my friends. Sure, I cared about my baby brother, but only when I was home and around him. I know that's selfish but, I was busy being a teenager.

Much of my free time was taken up with dancing. I started modern jazz at the Santa Monica Dance Studio when I was very young. As a teenager I convinced my dad to drive my girlfriends and me to Perry Park dances, and to Knott's Berry Farm to go to Cloud 9 and Studio K. When I was visiting my mom in the Palisades, before she moved to Redondo Beach, I went to the night club 321 in Santa Monica to dance on weekends, and to Peanuts in Hollywood. Peanuts was my favorite because it was a gay nightclub and I could dance all night and not be hit on by one creepy guy. What a relief that was, especially since I wasn't even old enough to be in the club.

Unfortunately, when I wasn't dancing, at school, or with my friends, I had to go home, and Alex didn't make my home life any better. I especially tried to not be home when my dad was out of town. That way my stepmonster could enjoy my baby brother. After all, she was a new mom and Alex wasn't even one-year-old yet. If I wasn't home we wouldn't argue, and I could hang with my friends for most of the weekend. Anywhere else was better than being verbally abused or neglected at home.

I loved being at a friend's house or out doing things, but my stepmonster used to ground me for the littlest thing—and I mean anything. She even made things up just to ground me. I mean fuck lady, I'm sorry. I'm breathing. I'm so sorry but I can't stop. Oh yeah, that's part of being human.

Once, I was at a girlfriend's house on a Saturday night on one of my mom's weekends. Three of us were going to spend the night and the next day we were going shopping at the South Bay Galleria, close to where one of the girls lived. One girl received a call from Greg's best friend, who wanted to hang out with us and meet us at the Galleria. The next day the girl whose house we stayed at decided she didn't feel like going shopping, so my other friend and I went.

When we got to the mall we ran into Greg, and a friend of his named Scott. And, let's be clear, not Scotty. I was thinking, oh God, why? Then I realized the meeting had been orchestrated. I was not thrilled, but I didn't want to bum out my girlfriend, because she clearly liked Scott. I must admit he was super sweet. So, I had to hang out with Greg and was stuck.

Recently, he had gotten a leather jacket and changed the way he dressed. He also had spiked his black hair. When he looked down at me with big, blue, puppy dog eyes, even though I had a boyfriend, he definitely caught my attention. But, I didn't date boys who went to high school. My boyfriend had a motorcycle, and was eighteen.

The guys had their flasks filled with booze and were on a mission to make the day as exciting as possible, in an effort to win us over. After shopping, the guys invited us to their house, which was super convenient because Greg lived across the street from my mom. I thought, *this is great. Now I have a ride home.* This also worked out because my mom worked nights, so when I was there I didn't have to deal with her continued frustration and anger. Another result of the aneurysm was that I had quickly learned how to survive and be on my own.

Many decades later, Mom remains paralyzed on one side. Her leg swings outward when she walks, her arm is paralyzed, and her hand is frozen into a fist. For a number of years, she worked as a telephone operator in the hotel business.

When I found out that neither of the guys we were with had a car I asked, "How do you expect us to get to your house?" They looked at each other, then talked us into walking, explaining that we were on an adventure, and by the way, there is LSD in that whiskey you're drinking.

Wait. What?

We decided to walk, and it didn't seem that far, but walking took so much longer than driving. Just when we were getting tired and I was thinking this adventure sucked, the acid kicked in. We walked from the South Bay Galleria down Inglewood Boulevard. Then we came across the Rice Cemetery and Greg suggested we go in and check it out.

How did I get talked into this? I couldn't even watch a horror movie and now I was going into a cemetery while tripping on acid.

Let the adventure begin. While I acted cool, inside I was scared, especially because I had never taken any kind of a drug before. There is a first time for everything I guessed, and this *was* the eighties.

The guys loved scaring us, and running through the cemetery making us jump and cling to them. I really was scared, and was clinging onto Greg as if he could save me from it all. We finally made it to my mom's after all the drugs calmed down, and I invited them in, since my mom was at work. That's when Greg asked me to sit on his lap, where he kissed me for the first time. That's how I met my first love in high school.

You may ask why I fell for a guy who gave me drugs without my knowledge or my consent. At the time I thought it was an adventure and he was cute! He had big blue eyes and I had the time of my life living on the edge—for a minute. Ultimately though, I've turned out to be super responsible.

Just then I heard a motorcycle engine. I heard it from blocks away, and then there was a knock at my door. My soon-to-be ex-boyfriend and my new boyfriend stood face to face in my house. All I can say is, I was busted! As you might imagine, it didn't go over very well with the soon-to-be ex. I honestly didn't mean to hurt anyone, but I did. It's not fun to be on either side of the fence, the cheater or the cheated. When the guys met face to face, there was a little yelling, especially towards me. I was grateful no one started fighting.

Finally, I introduced them, and as they looked each other up and down it was awkward. But, it was clear I had made my choice. As a high school freshman, it also was clear to me that I didn't like the way I was feeling. I'm an honest person and would have preferred to break my existing relationship off before entering into another relationship, or even had a kiss.

♥

One Saturday morning around nine or ten I got a ride home from my girlfriend's mom. I had spent the night there, and she had to go into work that day. I walked into my dad's house and down the hallway toward the kitchen where my stepmonster was with Alex and our housekeeper. I had to walk this way to get to the staircase to go down to the basement and garage. The basement bedroom was my room, and it was the farthest bedroom away from the "parentals." This was so the housekeeper/nanny could have my old room and Alex could have the room next to hers and be near his parents. That was fine with me because I could blast my music and talk on the phone with more privacy.

As I was walking to my bedroom, my stepmonster said something to me. Apparently she was mad because I had spent the night at my friend's house.

"But Dad said I could stay," I said. "I did ask permission."

It wasn't my fault if there was a lack of communication between them. It was always lame like that. Dad would want to be cool and she would talk him into grounding me. My feeling was that she should not be the boss of me, and that my dad was. In reality, she was the boss of us all. She definitely bossed my dad around. She couldn't find it in her heart ever to be nice, or remember that she was a teenager at once. You could see the hatred coming off her like a cartoon character blowing steam out of her ears.

In the middle of her yelling at me from the kitchen, the phone rang. Of course I went to answer the phone, but she beat me to it. One of my friends was on the line, and screaming at my friend, she told her I was grounded and cannot talk, then she hung up. My girlfriend was a junior and a little older than I was, and she called back to tell my stepmonster she was rude. My friend wasn't used to that type of behavior from an adult. It didn't help me out, but I'm glad my friend cared enough about her own self respect to not allow anyone to treat her that way.

As we argued, I continued to walk down the staircase to my room. This staircase was very steep, and with many stairs. My stepmonster pushed me from behind and I went face first flying down the stairs. Thank God I grabbed the railing half way down and caught my fall, because if I hadn't, I would have most likely broken my neck and died.

Then I ran back upstairs, chased her around the kitchen and living room, and that is when I got into my first fight—with a grown woman, a mother figure. I had two moms who claimed the title and both were bat shit crazy! Enough was enough. I was no longer going to take anymore of the abuse. I'd had enough of the yelling, enough of the unnecessary groundings. She didn't want me there and I was afraid she would try to kill me again. I was now in my middle teens, and was bigger and stronger than when she first married my dad. She now had a true fight on her hands.

In hindsight, I should have called child protective services. Instead, I decided to stick up for myself. Now I was in a full-on fist fight. My dad believed children did not have a voice next to an adult. It was such an un-evolved way of thinking. True old school, depression-type of thinking. So naturally, he believed her over me. Later, I often said to myself, "That crazy bitch will get her karma one day for sure."

After, my stepmonster gave my dad an ultimatum. Either I left or she would. My dad cried for three nights over this. I heard him each of those nights. I loved my dad. I was Daddy's little girl. We were buddies, so what the hell was going on? Why was life getting worse?

My dad eventually told me that if I went away it would be to attend a boarding school. Of course I didn't want to go, but I told my dad I would, only to get my mediocre grades up and to let things calm down. I knew my dad loved both me and his wife, and was stuck in the middle. I thought by me volunteering to go this would be an effort in good faith for getting along in the future. No big deal. I would go away, get a break, tackle a new experience, get my grades up, and come back to peace and harmony. We would all call a truce. Not even close!

On top of it all, I had to tell my friends and new boyfriend I was leaving for the rest of the school year. "It's just the school year," I told them. "I'll be back in the summer and back at Redondo High with everyone to start tenth grade."

Unfortunately, I believed my dad. I trusted him. Little did I know this episode would be the final straw that broke the camels back for me in the trust department. Thanks, Dad. Now I have Daddy issues.

Love Note

Dear Lady,

I have many things I've wanted to say to you over many years. When I was a child you took away my father and family from me. My father and I had a very healthy dad and daughter relationship before he fell in love with you. We tried to continue our racquet ball Sundays and other activities, but your selfishness of always putting yourself first before me, the child, his daughter, along with your constant ultimatums put so much pressure on my father. Your actions and behavior caused so much damage to so many people. The ultimatum of either you or me leaving hurt me, my father, our grandparents, aunts, uncles, and cousins, even my son.

    You took me, an adopted child, away from the only family I had known. You scared me and were extremely cruel to me as a child, and now that I am an adult you continue to be cruel and selfish when it pertains to me.

    I made a childish choice by walking away from my family, even the family members who always stood by my side. I walked away *thinking:* If I was gone for good and no one in our family ever saw me again, I was making the right, selfless choice. *By me removing myself I thought you wouldn't be angry anymore, and that would cause less stress on my family. They wouldn't be forced to choose, or be put in an uncomfortable situation.*

But, by me making that choice, I also hurt the people I loved. My son and I missed weddings, funerals, and babies being born. My son and I missed our family very much.

By the way, to be clear, this is my family, my father's side of the family, the family I was adopted into and raised with. Do you really love my father? I believe that if you really love him you could have been kind to his daughter. You could have acted like an adult.

My father and family should never have had to choose between other family members. My son and I should have always been in-cluded. Everyone should have been invited to family events. You and I, dear lady, do not ever need to be friends or consider each other as family. I know I can be in the same room with you, say hello, and keep moving. Can you do the same?

If just being in my presence makes you so angry, insecure, or jealous; and causes you to behave so childishly, not be able to con-trol your emotions or act like an adult at family functions, then that's something I hope you can find a way to work on.

I do want to thank you for being a good mother to my brothers. I do believe you love my dad. I do believe you know you made many mistakes and will have to deal with your own karma in your own way on your journey in life.

I hope and wish for you to not have so much hate in your heart, because hate brings illness.

The last thing I want to say to you is: I forgive you, I forgive you, I forgive you. I will say this everyday, until I truly can forgive you.

Sam

Valentine's Day

THIS BOARDING SCHOOL WASN'T really a boarding school at all. It was more of a juvenile placement home for kids under the age of eighteen who did time on their crime in juvenile hall, but were not ready to be released back into society. Some kids had to stay because they had no family or parents involved, and/or a court had ordered them to stay in a "house program." That was part of their pre-probation.

I had been sent there as the result of the fight I'd had with my stepmom that turned physical. There was only one other kid there who had the same circumstances as I did, and both of our parents had enough money to have us put into the program. I'm sure it was a hefty fee, just like at a private school or boarding school, and by the way, I would have taken either one of those over this place in a heart beat.

This place had barbed wire fencing that looked like a prison you might see on TV, locked down doors with those giant push bars, and a ten-minute shower was all anyone was allowed. Therapy was everyday, and sometimes twice a day. Our school was on campus and girls were not allowed purses, jewelry, tampons, etcetera. We ate when they fed us and there were tons of chores. Other than that there was nothing to do, and we all had to earn any type of privilege. I washed doors and walls just to get their so called "privilege," one of which was to be able to smoke cigarettes. Gross! I hate smoking but that was all there was to do. So, this is where I learned to smoke. Great place, Dad. Your parenting skills are on point. I still can't believe my adopted dad signed off allowing me, as a minor, to smoke cigarettes. If you can't beat them, join them. It turned out to be survival for me, and a way to fit in and be somewhat cool.

I actually had an angel in that place. (Thank God for my punk rock roots.) She was the baby sister of a guy I used to hang out with in the Suicidal Tendency days. BAE days! Before Anyone Else! Anyway, lil' sis was there and kept the lesbians, crazies, and bullies away from me. This was on instructions from her big brother. I was so grateful for Ava. Much love to her, and I hope life is treating her well and that she reads this one day. She will always be in my thoughts and heart. She protected me, stood next to me when I may or may not have had to fight my way out from the bigger, older chicks. Thank you, Ava!

I didn't belong there and she knew that better than anyone. What were the odds I'd have a second degree of separation in that crazy scenario? I'm sorry for the lock down I must have caused her and all the girls when I finally escaped. That was routine, to lock down the facility whenever anyone escaped, so the other girls all paid a price for me. I knew not to get caught or my ass would get a beat down from the other girls. A lock down was no fun for anyone.

After I left, I know all the girls raided my clothes and belongings. And you know what? I was cool with that because at least I left everyone with a little piece of me. Even in a so called prison I had my own little style. I hope Ali got my royal blue vest. (Ha ha.)

I had become somewhat friendly with a skinny girl named Amy while I was "kept captive," as I like to put it. She was a bit off, but always had everyone's best intentions at heart. I didn't like how people treated her. I'm not down with the bullying types, so the very long six months I spent in there I had her back. Then, because of Amy's good sense of awareness, she saw a window of opportunity and shared it with me.

"Sam," she said. "A car is going to leave at lunch and the gate is going to open right before it closes. Run!"

Amy and I moved to the very back of the line so we could go to lunch from school. I couldn't believe she was helping me. I hadn't discussed anything with anyone about wanting to run, or escape. I hadn't even confided in my roommate. I actually stayed in that fucked up place for six months so I could go on one outing with a group as a reward for good behavior, just so I knew where in Southern California I was.

On that outing I was on my best behavior, and did some bonding with the teachers so they would trust me. I quickly realized we were right off the National exit on the 405 freeway, just before it meets the I-10. Now, as soon as the gate started to close I could finally break out and escape this youth prison. The black car passed through the gate, and as the gate started to close, the line I was in started to walk and I ran out the gate. Free at last! I ran right around the corner and into the nearest restaurant.

I tried to catch my breath, but as soon as I looked up there were two teachers having lunch and I was face to face with them both. Holy shit! I was so scared, and I knew right then that this was the time for me to earn the best actress award! A life saving performance was on it's way, and the water works began. I knew I had to lay it on thick because I only had one shot. If I was sent back, I'd get my ass beat down by all the other girls. The thought of that alone was motivation enough.

I walked up to the teachers and said in full throttle of tears, "a boy broke up with me." The school was co-ed, and all teenage girls have a meltdown at some point over a boy. "You're my favorite teacher," I said to one of them. "I know I'm marked as AWOL now, but I just have to talk to you."

That's when I won my first and only acting award, because she said, "Honey, you know you're in a lot of trouble."

"I know," I said, "but I only can talk to you. You're the only one who understands me. I knew you were having lunch here."

Of course I lied. I had no idea they were having lunch there. My hands were flying everywhere to express my distress, along with the huge tears streaming down my face. See how boys can mess with our emotions?

The teacher told me to walk back to school and wait on the steps in back of the institution and in front of her classroom. They would pay for their lunch and handle the situation in five minutes. That in and of itself was odd. They should have grabbed me right then and marched me back. Maybe they were tired of me and wanted me to escape? Maybe they felt for me and knew I didn't belong in there? In any case, I was incredibly lucky that events played out as they did.

I sniffled and agreed to go back on my own, and walked out of the restaurant toward the institution. But, instead of going back, I ran to the back of the restaurant and jumped into a dumpster to hide. I soon heard sirens and knew they were searching for me.

To my surprise, I found I was not alone in the dumpster. No, I didn't see bugs or rats. What I saw in there was a male bum! What the F? Scared to death, I jumped out, risking all my efforts to escape. Fortunately, the dumpster was mostly filled with trash bags that had been tied tightly shut, so little of the trash had leaked onto me. I ran to the nearest clothing store and pretended to shop, as if I was older and out of school. Desperately, I was trying to keep it cool.

Meanwhile, I watched vans from my "prison" pass by, and I held my breath as I rummaged through clothes pretending to be a consumer and not a runaway. As soon as one vehicle was out of sight I ran to the next safe store. That day I went in and out of many different stores to hide.

Eventually, I ran all the way from the institution to Marina Del Rey, a distance of more than five miles. I felt like I ran through Watts, and some other pretty scary areas for a thirteen-year-old girl. This, with no money in my pocket and without a purse or an ID.

It hadn't been a planned thing to go AWOL that day; it was just a small window of an opportunity that oddly presented itself. I had on surfer shorts, sneakers, and a white T-shirt. I woke up that morning thinking about school, and the next thing I knew I was on a pay phone with Scotty. I had called him collect. Scotty, my old boyfriend Mark (who was older), and a girlfriend of mine signed up to help me. The three of them became my saving grace and the ones who helped me stay free.

After the call I jumped into a cab and Scotty told me to tell the cab driver to take me to my girlfriend's house. He and Mark would meet me there to pay the cab fare. On the way, the cab driver started to question me. He was just figuring out something was wrong when I got to my girlfriend's. By that time the cabbie was threatening to call the cops on all of us. It's funny now, but then I was running for my freedom and my life, and I was scared. Mark gave the cab driver a fake gold chain, and Scotty gave him a twenty-dollar bill and half a bottle of vodka. The cab driver let me go.

The day of my escape was Valentine's Day. I still give thanks to all of my friends who helped save my ass. My ex-boyfriend even helped after I had been shitty to him and we had broken up. Scotty and my girlfriend knew I would have to disguise myself to walk around Redondo Beach without being recognized. My girlfriend put so much make up on me, I even had a spider web drawn on one of my eyes. My hair was black and down to my butt, so we wrapped it up in a bandana.

Late that afternoon we walked from my friend's house to the bus stop, and as we were walking on 190th, my adopted mom drove by and waved to Scotty. OMG! It was amazing, but she didn't recognize me. Thank God I was safe for a little longer. Next thing I knew, Scotty had us on a bus to Long Beach, to a club called Fenders Ballroom.

This was my very first punk show, and Scotty still has the original flyer from that. It was definitely a night to remember, especially because this was the night I met all the Carson and Wilmington crews. So many of us came together from many different cities and became family that night.

Life on the run was a surreal experience, but not one I was totally unprepared for. As I was growing up I had always been shipped off to summer camps. When I was younger I loved Cali Camp in Topanga Canyon, but as I grew older and my stepmonster became involved, camp wasn't a fun place anymore. Instead, it became a "ship her away for as long as we can" kind of thing.

One year my dad sent me away to my stepmonster's cousin's camp in West Virginia. Her cousin was the owner of the camp and this was the first time I had flown by myself. I was twelve. I flew into Washington, DC and was met by a twenty-year-old counselor guy who I had never met before. Honestly, I was scared to be with a stranger in an old beat-up pickup truck. I drove with this guy for about three hours. Once I got to camp I realized I was the only kid from California—and I had to stay there for two months. That was practically the entire summer.

While I was not happy to be there, the grounds of the camp were absolutely gorgeous and lush. My favorite part of West Virginia was when it was hot, and I blasted music and danced in the rain with my boom box. West Virginia was beautiful, but very far from my friends and from California. In California I sometimes went to Catalina Island Camp. This camp I loved, but it was still hard to be away from home. I went to that camp for a few summers, until I got too old to go.

Turned out all of that alone time, with the added experience of camp and my travels, had given me the strength and skills I needed to get through life. Looking back, even though I had no choice as to where I was sent, those experiences taught me how to survive. I now knew how to trust my instincts and that came in handy while I was hiding. I can't believe those scary summer camp experiences taught me how to read people, travel, and be on my own.

During camp I also got to know myself. I learned many social skills, and how to make new friends no matter what part of the world someone lived in or language anyone spoke. I learned to speak up and have a voice, ask questions, and most of all, how to be confident. Everyone gets those butterfly feelings in their stomach when nervous or excited. That's what I call a "healthy fear." I believe fear is false, mostly, but those butterfly feelings are a person's intuition, physically telling them to be aware of their surroundings or guiding them to safe ground.

Those camp years also taught me to listen to my intuition. Whenever I don't listen, something bad happens. I'm quick to learn, especially when something I try doesn't feel right. If something doesn't feel right, I get myself out of that situation pretty fast and go on to my next thing, one that hopefully does feel right. My feelings, and knowing myself (and who I am and what I want in life) was fully developed at a young age. I have always been driven and motivated, and was maybe a little too independent at age thirteen.

After my escape, I stayed at my girlfriend's house during the day and with Scotty at night. Scotty lived so close to my mom that I was scared I would get caught at his house. I went back and forth like this for two to three weeks until one afternoon when my girlfriend called my dad to tell him where I was. She felt I had been on the run long enough, and I'm sure her mom was starting to wonder what was going on.

I felt pissed and betrayed by her action. How could she do that to me? When my dad and I finally saw each other I told him if he ever sent me back to that place he would lose a daughter for life. My dad agreed, but that was when he still cared. His decision terrified my stepmonster to no end, and she said if I came back to their house she would divorce him. Little did I know then, that this would be the pattern of my relationship with my adopted dad for the rest of my life: he chooses to care about me and my stepmonster lays down an ultimatum.

Of course I wasn't going back to my dad's house. No way! Never in a million years would I have lived in that house again. I decided to move in with my mother for the first time since she moved to Redondo Beach. This was a great game plan. She worked nights and I went to school during the day. We barely saw each other and this was the only thing that kept us getting along.

Well, there were two things that helped us get along. One was that my adopted mom adored Scotty, as much as if he was her actual son. He had a way with her that was genuine and helpful. They became very close, almost as if he was her son and my brother. Scotty ended up living with my mom along with me—and after me. I don't know how we managed it but half the time we lived at his dad's and the other half we lived with my mom. We could walk to both houses, which helped because neither of us were old enough to drive yet. The emotional level of the various parentals was our deciding factor on where we were going to stay. As long as I was with Scotty, or he was nearby, I felt safe. He was the only person I could truly count on.

The other thing that helped us get along was that, in general, I had a lot more freedom to be with my friends. These friends soon became like family, as I could always count on them.

Back in school, I was ready to give tenth grade a go, ready to get back to my friends and try to have a normal high school experience. What is a normal high school experience anyway? Going back to school, well that kind of sucked. I had gotten used to hiding out and hanging out, so I was having a hard time getting back into the rhythm of school work. Then I saw him. New boyfriend, Greg. I can't believe that after my escape, going to punk shows, getting caught, moving to my moms, and living across the street from him, that I didn't think of him once. I didn't even think I had a boyfriend. I didn't expect him to wait around for me and I'm pretty sure he hadn't, but that changed when he saw me.

My life at this point was all over the place, and I was just starting to settle in. But all it took was a little conversation and one hang out after school, and that was it: my first, real, in-love, crazy high school, these two may get married kind of love. We were so serious, and I'm sure all of our parents were terribly afraid that there would be an early pregnancy. I think Scotty was worried about that, too. I was so pleased when Scotty and Greg became friends, real friends, true friends. But, Scotty always said, "that's my sister and my loyalty lies with her." When it came to Scotty, Greg always knew where he stood.

It was important to me that anyone I dated get along with my brothers. Older and younger brothers. Yes, another little baby brother coming soon! While my stepmonster was pregnant with my soon-to-be baby brother Davey, while she was picking out her baby's name, I was playing house with Greg. Here I was, fourteen and fifteen years old, picking our way down the line of future baby name. I spent the night with Greg all the time. We were always cuddled up on the couch watching movies and making out. I was, we were, madly in love.

One day several years later we watched the movie *The Crow*. The actor who played that roll was Brandon Lee, Bruce Lee's son, and his character's name was Eric Draven. I loved the name so much, and so did Greg's little sister, who was a few years younger. Right then and there his sister and I made a pact that when we grew up and had children we would each name our first born Draven. It didn't matter if we had a boy or a girl, our first-borns were going to be named Draven. We all had our hearts deeply vested to this name.

Greg was a deep person who also was a bit on the crazy side. At times he did very stupid things to get attention. Honestly, he wasn't the only one. There was a crew of us that hung at the Hermosa Pier and charged tourists money to take our photos so we could have booze money. There were a lot of tourists in California, especially at the beach, and all of us were Punk AF (Punk As Fuck). Liberty spikes, leopard animal prints, and twin Mohawks with death locks. I had hot, flamingo fuchsia Manic Panic-dyed hair down to my butt.

All of us wore hand-made gear, including leather jackets with safety pins, studded up in spikes, and colored with amazing paintings that we either did ourselves or had friends who were tattooists paint. I had diamond and heart studs on my leather, and I also had my Docs (Dr. Martens) with the heart and diamond studs to match my leather. But, I always took Scotty's leather every chance I got. His was bigger and far more comfortable. It was also more worn, so was way cooler than mine. I probably wore Scotty's jacket more than he did.

Greg was damn dramatic, or was always caught up in trying to be so "punk rock." And, he always said that he was going to die at the age of twenty-one. At first when he started to share those statements I dismissed them. I knew Greg loved attention, but after awhile it bothered me so very much that he said those things. Greg didn't have depression, and was the kind of guy whom everyone liked. All this death talk was such a negative bummer to me. I absolutely love life, so to hear someone you love remind you that he is predicting he will die at the early age of twenty-one was starting to wear on my nerves.

We actually fought regularly over this, amongst other things. But for Greg, it was more like a premonition rather than a desire to die. Greg loved life as much as I did. He just had a calm feeling that twenty-one would be his time. He spoke about it often to Scotty and me as if he had found peace with it, and we both got so irritated over it.

One Thanksgiving night Scotty and I joined Greg and his family. I showed up late from visiting my dad, and everyone was waiting for me. Greg gave me a hard time and we got into a big fight. I walked in, got into an argument, and turned right around to walk back down the stairs to leave. Scotty told Greg to calm down and gave him a moment to talk with me alone, to find out what was up, but before we could speak, Greg started screaming in a passionate fit of jealousy, so I left the house. High school drama!

Outside, Greg grabbed me to turn me around to talk to him. He must have realized that I'd had a rough afternoon. When I get pushed too hard emotionally, I shut down. From an early age, my mom and dad told me that I was biologically Italian on my father's side and Greek on my mother's, so when I'm mad I speak my mind. Then, 98 percent of the time, I let it go and it's over. It's safe to say that when I speak my mind, or if I scream and yell, it's better, after. It's rare, however, if I ever get that mad, for me to raise my voice. I start to sound like Penélope Cruz in the movie *Blow*—without the blow! I say what I feel, and then let it go. If I'm upset and quiet, that's when people should be afraid, because I'm calculating my next move.

On this particular evening, I yelled back and was walking to my adopted mom's house when Greg grabbed me, and my favorite necklace, the one with my gold charms, broke. I wore this necklace every day, and it meant a great deal to me. One charm was a baby ruby ring that I had gotten from my adopted mom's grandfather, my papa Joe. My charms also included a floating heart that I received from my grandma, and a symbol of an "S," all in gold, that my dad gave me. I was shocked and devastated when my necklace broke.

Greg, Scotty, Greg's sister and I all spent hours searching for my charms in the bushes, on the nearby lawn, and even in the cracks of the sidewalk. We had flashlights and were intensely searching. Two of the three missing charms we found: my floating gold heart and my baby ring. But, my "S" charm was forever gone. I was so heartbroken that this was the end of Greg and me. How dare he! I know it was an accident, but I needed a real man, not a little boy who was going to create drama and allow jealousy to control his every move.

I realized at a young age that I loved passionately and did everything with 200 percent. I'm such a free spirit. I learned with my first love that I would always drive every future boyfriend crazy, because they could not own or control me. Their best bet was to understand and protect me, and to give a splash of encouragement and a ton of support so we could uplift each other.

I always could see "the special" in others, even when they could not see it themselves. Greg was on a destructive path, and his parents were concerned for him, so shortly after the Thanksgiving incident he moved from Redondo Beach to Tennessee to live with his father. This actually made me sad and happy all at the same time. I knew the move was the best for Greg, and would be best for me, too. We could both spread our wings and learn to fly, and if we were meant to be then we would find each other and get back together. Doesn't that sound romantic?

To be honest, we all could have used a little more self control back then. I'm not passing judgment on anyone, and that includes myself. I really believe that if it's meant to be, it will be. I do not believe in coincidence. In my mind we are all connected in the same energy, so we have purpose. Little did I know that on the night of Thanksgiving, when I lost my "S" charm, Greg found it and kept it for himself. Shortly after Greg moved he found a new girlfriend, graduated high school, then moved to Kentucky to attend college. He had his heart set on culinary school. I actually liked hearing updates about Greg's life through Scotty. I was happy for him when I heard he was engaged, and when Scotty told me the news that Greg had passed at the age of twenty-one, I was in shock.

By this time I was eighteen and was in the middle of moving to San Clemente, California. One of my friends had moved there and I was caught up with the wrong group of people. I thought moving, and being in a different environment, would be healthy and put me on the right path. I wanted to be on the path of success. Not the path I was currently on, hanging out with not the best of people. I was young and struggling to pay bills and survive. While I was figuring it out I hung around "low hanging fruit."

But, I couldn't leave South Bay without saying goodbye to Scotty. A girlfriend was helping me move and we popped in for a quick goodbye, because it was really just bye for now. When we walked in, Scotty asked me to sit down as he had something to tell me.

I don't believe I actually sat down, but when Scotty told me Greg was gone, I do remember thinking he was pulling a prank on me. I actually got mad at him for making something like that up, even though I knew Scotty was not a liar. I just didn't want to hear what I had just heard.

A girlfriend and I went to Greg's mom's house, but no one was home. After a phone call or two, a plan was made for me to go visit his family at a pre-arranged day and time. On the assigned day, I went to spend an afternoon with his mom and sisters. I watched the video of Greg's funeral, and saw the paperwork from the hospital along with Greg's x-rays. On the x-rays and around his neck was a necklace with my "S" charm. OMG! "My charm!" I screamed. His mom told me he always wore it, that he had always loved me. There was shocker number two.

I moved to San Clemente shortly after, and after staying with a girlfriend exactly one month, a one bedroom opened up. Anthony Chapa was my current boyfriend. We met through mutual friends when I was sixteen and he and I weren't doing so well with this long distance relationship thing. I love space and independence—but not too much. Out of sight out of mind. I am a social butterfly, but there's a lot within my free spirit and Sagittarius nature for some to handle.

Eventually, Anthony moved to San Clemente to be close to me. We both knew we needed to hustle between work and both of us were in school. Anthony worked at Kragen Auto Parts while I worked, first at a clothing store, then at a three-day mini-blind store while I also managed an apartment complex. Anthony was getting ready to go to medical school and I was getting ready to go to cosmetology school and then real estate.

I wasn't sure what I wanted to do now that I was eighteen and on my own. I knew if I wanted to attend any type of school or college I would also have to work my ass off for money to pay for food, rent, utilities, and other bills.

I approached the owners of the condo in the triple triplex we rented (three buildings with three units apiece in them) and asked if I could be their on-site property manager in exchange for free rent. My attitude of what the heck do I have to lose paid off, and this became a surprisingly good win-win situation for me, as well as for the property owners. Then I enrolled in cosmetology school. The mini-blind store that I worked in after class was next to the school. It was convenient, and I had my plate full with school, two jobs, and a fiancée. Oops, I skipped that part. Yes, Anthony and I got engaged.

One night I woke up to several Marines yelling their usual drunk, obnoxious words as they walked past our house from the nearest local bar. We lived near Camp Pendleton, so there were always Marines around. We also lived across the street from Trestles, one of the hottest local surf spots.

This particular group of Marines were so loud, when I looked over at Anthony, I couldn't believe he was still sleeping. I was getting pretty mad by this point, so I got out of bed and walked to the edge of my bed and when I looked at Anthony, I also saw myself sleeping. What the heck? I looked down at my feet, and saw they were floating at the edge of my bed but not touching the floor. A very calm feeling washed over me, and I had zero fear.

The laughter grew louder, and I followed it because it started to sound familiar. I now realized there were no Marines outside my house and I followed the familiar laugh all the way to Redondo Beach, to Greg's mother's house. I went through the living room, the kitchen, up through the staircase, and into Greg's old room, which was empty. Then I floated into his sister's room, then his mother's room. I saw everyone sleeping, and the next thing I knew I was on a sidewalk and then in a townhome I had never seen before.

I went inside and up to a loft and sat down. Then I leaned back into Greg's arms. Was I dreaming? It felt so real. Greg looked exactly how I remembered, and we spoke without words. Then I heard a distorted voice. It wasn't like a computer voice, but it wasn't human either. The voice gave me a choice. It asked if I wanted to stay with Greg, or go on living the way I was. Basically, I had a choice to go on to the next realm, or finish out my current journey.

I don't remember consciously making a choice. I just remember waking up and gasping for air, grabbing my arms and body, checking to see if I was alive or not. Some say I had an out of body experience, but I truly believe I was given a choice. It was more than just a dream.

There were so many things I had wanted to ask Greg. His family told me he was found face down, beaten to death, floating in the Kentucky River. They said actress Sharon Tate's mom was the psychic on the case. He was murdered? Why? He was only twenty-one years old. Why did Greg always tell us he would die at twenty-one? What happened? Did he have a premonition when he was a kid? Did he manifest this? Why did he have to die? I wish I could have seen him one last time. Just once.

After I woke up, I was very sad. I had no control over what happened in my out of body experience. It was as if I had been guided. I followed Greg, or should I say, I followed his laughter, then I ran into who I would say was, "Source" or "God," and then poof, I was pushed back into my body. I have not had an out of body experience since, which I think is good, as the entire experience was hard for me emotionally. I had never before lost someone I loved so much, especially someone so young. I remember thinking that no parent ever should have to bury their child.

I also couldn't remember actually making my choice. I must have made one, though. For months I missed Greg terribly, and had to keep it bottled up all to myself. After all, I had a fiancé and was getting married soon.

Where the Devil Lives

ANTHONY AND I EVENTUALLY got married. We were young and thought we were in love. Anthony wanted to attend medical school in Arizona, so as soon as I graduated from cosmetology school, we relocated to the Phoenix area. Even though several friends of ours moved to Arizona with us, living there was a shell shock for me. So much so that I flew home to Los Angeles to visit Celine and my friends thirteen times in one year. Thank goodness for cheap Southwest flights.

At that age I felt I could do anything. The sky was the limit. When I look into the sky I do not see a ceiling, and I always go for everything I want, can dream about, or even imagine. At a very young age I knew exactly how to manifest my dreams. Now, I was learning a new profession, and new skills, all with major financial gain.

I was job hunting, and went on an interview for a receptionist for a new developer and property owner from Calgary, Canada. Oh yes, I got the job! I was so excited. To be a part of a new start up development company and work for a property owner who was deep into the real estate game was extremely exciting to me. Especially since my only experience in the field was managing three triplexes.

My new boss took a chance on me and trusted me, and that gave me a huge sense of purpose. Doug, my boss, was incredibly supportive and provided training classes anytime I wanted or needed them. He knew the classes would help me grow within the company, and as an individual. So, I went to every class and attended every course I could. My favorite was a time management class. It was one of the first classes I attended, and served me the most. Since then I've always felt I can run circles around most people in how I manage my time. For that alone, I have a huge amount of gratitude to that class, and for Doug. He always pushed me to be the best I could be, and helped me learn as much as possible. Wow, a real chance at a career and education that would serve me throughout my life. I quickly worked my way from receptionist to assistant vice president to Mr. Doug Edgelow. Doug was the greatest boss ever.

Eventually I found myself on the board of directors of several communities that he owned, or sometimes, owned several units in a building. Other times it was an entire condominium complex. When a company owns so many units and there is a homeowner's association someone had to assume a larger vote, and being involved and on the board as a member was necessary. I never told Doug this, but I was terrified to speak to a crowd. So, I had to get comfortable speaking in front of large crowds immediately. Fake it till you make it, right!?

As Doug's assistant, I climbed the ladder every chance I got, and took places on boards, which relieved Doug from having to attend the once a month evening meetings several times a week. This showed my commitment and dedication. Plus, after work all day and an HOA meeting at night, well, that made for long days but a great paycheck. Finally, I was working my way to a nice salary. Doug owned so many properties and was a part of so many communities. From Section 8 housing to custom homes in Cave Creek, Phoenix, Tempe, Paradise Valley, and Scottsdale, I literally was on every board.

It didn't take me long to learn what hat to wear and role to play when it came to business. I managed twelve or more properties at one time, plus refurbishing, new builds, and land he was purchasing, financing, mortgages, escrow, etcetera. Doug even gave me an employee discount and helped me purchase my first home at the age of twenty-two. I was very blessed to have an honest male role model who wasn't creepy!

But, Anthony and I had marital problems that were growing by the minute. I had never been married before so didn't know what I was doing. I'm not sure either of us knew what we were doing. In that thought, of course we were bound to have marital problems. It was hard enough to be so young and married. At the beginning we also did not know how financial pressures can strain a marriage, but we soon found out.

To add to the pressures that flowed into our marriage was my new job. I was gone a lot of hours. It became hard for me because I had a full on demanding career that I loved, and that's where I wanted to be. It all was worth it, though. One day I realized I wasn't flat broke anymore! I was a boss, and a very young one at that. I didn't want to have children or buy real estate with Anthony, because I saw us growing apart. I wanted to grow up, and I had big dreams. I was so hungry and ambitious, but my husband was still partying with his friends. Even though we were married, our life together was rocky and I wasn't sure where our future was going to take us.

I was in charge of hiring and scheduling many vendors, and had hired a carpet company to remove and replace carpets for several of our properties. That is when I met Joey. Joey and his carpet-cleaning crew were amazing, efficient, and complete professionals and Joey became my first real friend, someone who I could relate to while I lived in Arizona. We became great friends not only for our love of punk rock, but for our passion for life.

I hoped Anthony could meet Joey, but he had zero interest. He also had his friends from work, including his best friend and his friend's girlfriend, both of whom who made the move with us. Anthony definitely wasn't interested in meeting anyone I worked with––especially a guy who was a total cutie pie. Joey and I worked together a lot so it became easy for us to develop our friendship. I pinky swear on my life we were and always have been just friends. For God sakes, I was married!

After work was not a good time for me to hang out, because Anthony was a bit on the jealous side, and me being a social butterfly always pissed him off. Most people after work grabbed drinks with their co-workers. But, the only one I could do that with and get away with it was my boss. Anthony and I lived in the townhome that I wanted to buy that my boss, Doug, had offered an employee discount. But, I knew to wait until Anthony and I figured out our marriage. I really needed to purchase the property, but only when the time was right. We were able to stay in the townhome for free as a bonus to my salary, and I was on the board of directors for the complex. I managed about twenty-two units at this community—until we sold them one by one.

♥

Over the years I had become more curious about my biological family and decided to try to find them. I started by calling adoption services and the hospital where I was born. Before long I had the information I needed. No one in my family admitted to knowing who my biological parents were, but I always suspected my dad knew. I don't know why; I guess it's just my intuition. My cousin Celine came to visit me in Arizona often, but on one trip, after finding my biological mother, she and I decided to make the trip to Michigan to meet my birth mom and her family. This break, hopefully, would also be healthy for Anthony and me.

Celine and I were off to meet the Greeks! I was so nervous, and I know she must have been as well. Celine and I were going to stay with my bio mom, her husband, and my baby brother and sister. All I could think about was what it was going to be like being around blood relatives—people I physically resembled.

The trip was wonderful. Turns out my biological mom is 100 percent Greek, and very beautiful. I also met my grandparents, and many aunts, uncles, and cousins—and my siblings. I even met some of my mom's best friends who she grew up with. My mother got pregnant with me at the age of fifteen and gave birth to me at sixteen. This is a story a lot of people can relate to. The way my mom told me the story was, she wanted to hang out with her older brothers, and like any normal older brother they didn't want their baby sister hanging around and being in the way. This dismissal gave my mom the full opportunity to hang with the Italian guys across the railroad tracks. All kids that age want to hang out with their friends, or other kids. Not to mention the cute bad boys across the railroad tracks!

My mom ended up hooking up with an Italian guy named Benny, and in approximately nine months, I was born. I was extremely grateful that my mom had me, and didn't have an abortion. I'm not sure what her options were back in the seventies. I was born in 1971, and being pregnant and having a baby at the age of sixteen, well it was a total sin! Especially as my mom was Orthodox Greek and the father was an Italian Catholic from the wrong side of the tracks.

My grandparents shipped my mom off to Florida for the pregnancy, and for my birth they brought her back to Michigan. The family calls my grandfather Papu, which means grandpa in Greek.

My papu really wanted me to go to a good family, and even though Benny's mom, my Italian grandmother, wanted me, my papu knew I would be better off being adopted, than having my biological father trying to raise me from in and out of prison.

When we arrived at my grandparents, it was a party with all the family members. For me, it was just like the good times before all hell broke loose when I was seven. I remember thinking how handsome and beautiful my grandparents were, and their rich zest for life was so much fun! I immediately fell in love with them, and with my entire biological family. Everyone was so close and loving. I prayed they would accept me. I looked so much like my siblings, especially in our baby pictures, and I thought that was the coolest part.

My mom, Celine, and I stayed up talking one night, and she told me how she loved red licorice. This stuck with me, because oddly enough, that's my favorite candy as well. She told me that she knew where I was, and once when she was in California with her best friend she said she sat in a car, watching me play on the playground at elementary school. She said she was curious, but didn't want to disturb me. She also said she held me in the hospital until a social worker took me out of her arms. That was the last time she had contact with me, until now.

My mom also filled me in on my biological father, and explained he was always into trouble or on drugs. She was afraid of him interrupting her life with her new family, and I didn't blame her at all. I was very appreciative that she shared as much as she did. Her husband, who is the father of my brother and sister, is a wonderful man! I'm so happy for my mom. They are a very close and loving family, and I didn't want to disrupt that. I only wanted to be a part of it.

I may be my mother's first born, but I represent a past that she didn't want anything to do with. She made it very clear that she wanted nothing to do with Benny, and I wasn't even that curious about him. I knew deep down inside that desire would surface eventually, but then, I didn't have a curious bone in my body. I recognized the fear she had because of my past. I only wanted to know if I had siblings from his side, and some medical history for when I had my own children. My mom told me if I ever wanted to know more about my father, just to call Johnny, her best friend. I thought she said that because she didn't want to be involved if I ever chose to find him.

Celine and I went out one night with Johnny, and we even met up with some of my adopted cousins. We were twenty-one and twenty-two, and wanted to get out to party. My cousin Brad is my aunt Jackie's son. She is my a.k.a. mom. Brad was DJ'ing at the club we went to that night. Before we got there, though, Johnny took Celine and me down memory lane. He even drove us by the house I was conceived in! It was really overwhelming.

Turns out my papu was friends with an attorney who knew a couple in California who were looking to adopt a baby. A friend of the attorney was married to my adopted grandfather's sister, and their niece is Jackie Kallen, who has always been a loving aunt and pseudo-mother to me. Jackie has two sons, Brian and Brad, who were raised with me. Jackie wanted a baby girl in addition to her sons, and always said she wanted to adopt me. But her uncle, the attorney, had promised me to the California family.

While not related, Jackie was best friends with my adopted parents, so our families were totally intertwined. As a matter of fact, Jackie was the woman who posed as the social worker, and was the woman who took me out of my mother's arms. I love it when Jackie shares this story, because she makes me feel so loved and wanted.

Jackie has always been a mother to me in the truest sense, and has been the greatest woman role model any little girl could ask for. Having Jackie in my life was truly a blessing from God. She taught me everything a mother should be, including how to do business in a man's world and having the balance a woman needs to be loving and strong. I'm extremely proud and honored to have such a loving role model. I may not have had the best parental units, but having Jackie in my life completely filled the empty holes with love. I wanted to be exactly like Jackie. I knew, of course, that I would be me, and the events I experienced in life would shape me, but not define me.

Jackie was the first female manager in the sport of boxing, and made quite a name for herself there. She was also a show business journalist for a magazine in the 1970s, and interviewed artists such as the Rolling Stones, Frank Sinatra, Elvis Presley and many other amazing artists. It wasn't until my divorce from Anthony that I discovered, like mother like daughter, that the music business was also what was in store for me. She taught me well.

Overall it was a great trip, but when Celine and I got home life was not that much better with Anthony. Same old, same old, but now something had changed inside me. I wanted more in life. A fire had been lit within me.

Not long after, Anthony, my adopted dad, my cousin Brad, and I went to a huge fight in LA. One of Jackie's fighters, James Tony, was competing. I'm not a huge sports fan, but the way I was raised we had a lot of boxing, the LA Lakers, and the LA Kings. What do we cheer in Los Angeles? Go Kings Go! In my opinion boxing is one of the most glamorous sports. It was awesome to get all dressed up to attend the event, and people were decked out to the nines. The after parties were the icing on the cake. My dad knew Jerry Buss and his wife, owners of The Forum Club, a multi-purpose indoor music venue that is the "home court" in the Inglewood area of Southern California, and is mainly used for the Lakers.

In the evenings the arena turns into a concert hall. I was there all the time with my dad for Laker games. This is where I fell in love with basketball. I went with my dad whenever I could, and was always allowed to bring a girlfriend. I often ended up hanging out with other people who were there. Before the game, between games, after the games, and behind the scenes: having dinner parties with Funk artist Rick James (who first performed the song "Super Freak"), learning how to moon walk with Jermaine Jackson, or hanging out with Magic Johnson. Being around celebrities was normal to me; they're normal people who just have different talents or jobs. I actually thought this was all normal. Why wouldn't it be? We are all human.

Approximately a year later my biological mother and family, and my adopted dad and family, all decided to meet in Vegas. Quite the reunion, wouldn't you say?! What that meant was both sides of grandparents, both sides of parents, both sides of siblings, and biological cousins. That was a pretty heavy situation. I even had my stepmonster there. That always, every time, hands down, left a trace of damage. She was so evil and spoke so poorly about me to my biological mom. Well, to everyone, for that matter.

Unfortunately, my adoptive mom was not included in this event—or any other event that involved my dad, for that matter. It was as if she was an outcast. Even when it came to me, my adoptive parents never played nice. Other than the absence of my mom, it was a great time over all, and there were enough of us to keep my stepmonster and me separated with the least amount of interaction as possible. I thought things were pretty special for all of us to try to come together. I was excited. My bio mom and I were developing a little bit of a relationship!

Love Note

Dear Mom,

I want to tell you in case we never speak again that I'm so grateful you gave me life. I have so many things I want to thank you for, and I want to express all of it whenever you choose. It was a selfless act to choose to give me life, to give me to another family, and not have an abortion.

I can only imagine the fear, and the courage you had at such a young age. I only have love for you, and know that no one but you can ever understand what you went through.

Thank you, too, for the opportunity to know my biological family, to see that I look like other people, and for giving me enough info to have met Benny and my other side of my family. I know that was difficult for you and you were very angry with me for wanting to know where I came from. I didn't mean to hurt you. I just needed to know for my son, health, and the honest fact of curiosity. I needed to know all the "what if's," and it was exactly the same way I felt about wanting to find you.

Also, you were right. Benny was pretty bad into drugs. Heroin, as a matter of fact. And, he was just as you described him, maybe even worse. I also want to tell you that I have two sisters on that side. One I'm super close to, the other I have never met, but I have spoken with her mom. My half-sister Christina and I have been in each other's lives since our twenties.

I also want to tell you that you have a grandson who is now seventeen. His name is Draven Sebastian Bennington. My sister has two beautiful daughters, and for the first time, my son and I have blood relatives. We are all healthy, loving, and spend lots of quality time together.

I hope one day I get to see you, my brother, sister, and the whole family. I also understand, if not. I wish you all the health and love for you and the entire family.

Love, your first born daughter,

Sam

5

Curiosity Killed the Cat

THINGS WERE GOING WELL until I became curious about my biological father and called Johnny to ask for help. Ultimately, my bio mom thought I went behind her back, while I thought I wasn't involving her because that was what she wanted. I thought I was being respectful. As a young adult I was trying to handle my business with as little involvement on her part as possible, showing her I could keep these relationships separated. I thought that would prove to her we wouldn't have conflict, and I could, at my discretion, get to know both sides of my biological families.

My cousin Brad, Jackie's son, is the one who finally found Benny. My cousin ended up calling all the jails in and around Michigan, until he found one having an inmate with the right first and last name. My biological father was in a prison in Jacksonville, Michigan.

One evening when Anthony and I were at our house our phone rang. Brad was calling to give me some news. He had found the prison Benny had been in for the past twenty years. Twenty years! To me, the thought of being institutionalized for twenty flipping years is insane.

To the best of my knowledge, Benny spent twenty years in prison for something he was innocent of. I have since heard that everything else Benny did in his life was bad, and he got busted for just about everything he did. My bio dad was a very sloppy criminal.

My bio mother had told me that one time, however, this one and only time, was different. Benny owed money to a woman, probably for drugs. Or, God knows what he got himself into. The woman used to show up at my grandmother's home, as that's where Benny stayed between his, "in and out" of jail time. The woman made a scene, and demanded her money (which she probably, rightfully was owed).

Benny asked her to leave so my grandmother wouldn't get upset or be disrespected. It was snowing on this specific day, and porches in Michigan can become extremely slippery—as can any area with below degree temperatures. As the woman was leaving she slipped, fell, hit her head on the porch, and died instantly. Benny was on probation for all the things he did prior to this terrible accident.

I'm not sure how much of an investigation there was, and do not have all the details, but it wasn't good for Benny. In the end, this woman's death sealed his destiny to spend twenty years behind bars. Karma always catches up to you, one way or another.

When Brad told me he had found my biological father, and told me which prison he was in, my heart sank. I didn't know what the next move for me was going to be. I just kept thinking: *I have a right to know where I came from. I have a right to know if I have any more brothers or sisters.*

I also knew I didn't want to disturb my bio mom, and I was afraid she was going to be mad at me. I'd already had a taste of her being upset with me for asking questions about my father, let alone meeting him. But I also knew I had to meet him. My soul still had a hole in it for not knowing him, or where I came from. I just needed to muster up some courage to call the warden of the prison.

Calling a warden was intimidating! But, the next morning I made a phone call to the head warden of the prison. I spoke with him and he was respectful and kind as he listened to my story. I explained I was adopted and had never met my biological father. The warden seemed concerned for my safety, and explained that my father had not been a very good man, and was always in a lot of trouble. He also explained that when a man spends two decades in a prison, they're changed for life. Repeatedly, he asked me not to see him.

"I want to speak with him," I said, despite his words. "After that I will make my decision. I do have a right to speak to my biological father."

Benny was on his way to being released within weeks for time served, so the warden granted my wish and allowed a phone call between the two of us. I remember thinking that was kind of the warden, because he could have forced me to visit in person. I also think he heard in my voice that I was serious, and would have flown out there to meet Benny, if that was the only way I could speak to this stranger who gave me life.

Allowing me to speak by phone first was smart. After all, who knew how the conversation would go? I'm extremely grateful to this warden, because he followed an open heart and allowed me to meet my bio dad in this safe and secure manner. If not for the warden facilitating the meet with Benny, I would have never known about my half-sister Christina.

Speaking to Benny for the first time and hearing his voice was surreal. I was a nervous wreck, and I'm pretty sure he was as well. I didn't know if he was going to accept me. I didn't know if he was going to bother me and ask me a bunch of questions about my mother. That topic was off the table, as far as I was concerned. I would never speak about my mother to Benny. My mother is and never will be his business again. That was all in the past. I wanted a relationship with both of my families, if possible, but at the end of the day I would always choose my mother. Bottom line: I was scared, and in over my head.

The conversation turned out to be pleasant, and short. Benny explained how much he loved me and couldn't believe how he had this opportunity to speak to one of his daughters. He was embarrassed that he was in prison and by the choices he had made, but still was "blessed." He told me I had two other sisters, and that we're all from different mothers. He also said he was being released in a few weeks, and if I came to visit, it would mean the world to him to finally meet me. Of course with me being so adventurous and curious, all I could think was, *Yes, I have to go meet him!* Sometimes my curiosity gets the best of me.

I convinced Anthony to go with me, because there was no way I was going all by myself to meet a man I'd never met before, even if he was my biological father. This man was still a stranger to me, and, he was a stranger who was just getting out of prison. I couldn't get over that fact. Benny was, and will always be, a felon. It was very important to me that Celine went with me to meet my biological mother, but for meeting my biological father I needed the strength and protection of my husband.

Anthony and I might not have been getting along, but we were trying to figure it out. His support at this particular moment gave me the strength to move through uncharted territory. This meant the world to me, and showed me he was trying to repair some damage to our marriage.

There is one thing I have to say about Anthony, the man was beautiful. He looked like a Latino Ryan Philippe. He was tall, and had high cheek bones and pouty lips. Anthony was always trying to build a better life, but was forever stuck between a thug life and a beach life. His parents wanted more for him, but his uncle provided drugs and women, and trouble was always close behind.

Anthony and I flew to Detroit the day Benny was released from prison. I had arranged for Brad to meet Anthony and me at the airport at the gate (this was back when you could still meet passengers there), and then we'd get our luggage and meet Benny near the baggage claim area. Finally, we'd all go to Brad's condominium in Ann Arbor. Brad was so kind to let Benny, Anthony, and me stay in the home that he had for college. Of course, he would allow Anthony and me to stay at his place anytime, but to host an ex-convict straight out of prison was asking a lot.

Brad knew that I didn't take shit from anyone, and that he could trust me. He knew I would take care of anything that went wrong or ended up broken. My cousin trusted me and knew how responsible I was. Brad lived his life loving without judgment, just as Jackie had raised us all to do.

When we arrived at the house, Brad left Benny and me so we could get acquainted with one another. I was about to be in my biological father's world. But, the night before I was to fly to meet Benny, my adopted dad called and asked me not to get on the plane. He said it was a bad idea, and that my biological mother and Grandfather Papu didn't want me to go. I should, he said, rethink the entire trip.

"If you get on that plane," my adopted dad said, "you will be disowned as your biological mother's firstborn child."

That hurt me deeply, because now she had abandoned me twice—and by her own choice. Sure, my grandparents helped in her youthful choice. I pass no judgment on any of them, but to make me choose between truth, knowledge, and my birth family as an adult with a fresh new beginning, well, it dramatically changed the dynamic.

I was young, and I was hurt. I was not going to let somebody who could throw me away so quickly, as if I didn't even exist, dictate who was in my life. Also, I came from the same cloth, the same blood line, so I didn't back down easily. I've been known to follow my feelings, and some think I have caused more harm by doing what my soul has guided me to do. These usually are people who take zero responsibility for their actions. I, instead, find the sunshine at the end of my road by following my intuition. My feelings pull at me. I'm passionate, and grateful for being aware of my emotions. I'm Greek and Italian. What do people expect? I'm a fire cracker. Sometimes it serves me and sometimes it hurts.

I was curious. Which side of my bio family did I resemble more? Would I have an opportunity to have a blood relative in my life, and have the unconditional bond that I so craved? I hoped also to meet my cousins, aunts, uncle, and sisters. No one should take the opportunity away from someone to heal, or to find out where they come from.

This is important to me, but I know that isn't the case with all adopted children. Some are at peace and have no desire to know who their biological families are. I, on the other hand, have always had a huge desire to know where I came from. I had been looking for my biological parents since I was thirteen years old. I even signed up for the Alma Society, an organization that helps children find their birth parents.

For years I hit one closed door after the other, mostly because I had a closed adoption. My dad always told me that when I was older he would help me search for my family. But, as the years went by and I asked him yet again, the answer was always the same. "Next year," he'd say. "When you're older." So, to be at this place in my life where I could meet both birth parents and see where all my "life encounters" ended up, well, that is a story in itself.

I bet you want to know what it was like seeing Benny for the first time. Well, it felt right out of a movie. In my movie, in my memory in my head, Anthony and I came down the escalator to the baggage area side by side. Halfway down I gave Anthony that look, the one that meant if anything went sideways we had each other's back, no matter what. I saw my cousin in the near distance full of smiles, and there was a group of unorganized Italians behind him. It is as if I could see the Italians scrambling from a mile away. The picture my mother painted for me was spot on.

My cousin had no idea we all would soon meet the morons behind him. I felt safe with Anthony's crazy ass by my side, and at that moment I felt more supported than ever. All of a sudden I realized no one was better rolling next to me at this point than my husband. Never ignore your gut feelings. #intuitions

We got off the escalator and I said hello to Brad. I turned to Benny and several friends who were with him, and gave my biological father a quick hug and hello. Everyone from his group was rushing, looking around, keeping an eye on all surroundings. One man said to grab the bags, and another kept a look out. It was all happening so fast, as if Benny was expecting company—or maybe new problems. Anthony, Brad, and I just followed their lead. The high paced energy started to give me anxiety; I had never experienced an intuitive fear from collecting my luggage from the airport before. This was on top of an uncertain feeling floating in the air. As we left the airport it was Brad, Anthony, Benny, one of Benny's friends, and me. I have no idea where the rest of the people went. I never saw those people again and was totally okay with that.

We dropped off Benny's friend at his house, and the rest of us set off to Ann Arbor to my cousin's place to get settled in. In a matter of hours, I saw that Benny being in prison for twenty years made it difficult for him to be free on the outside. Technology changes greatly in a short period of time. I was frustrated by the fact that Benny didn't know how to use a microwave or a cordless telephone. I never thought that would be one of the challenges I would face in getting to know my dad. I certainly hadn't thought this through all the way.

Benny wanted us to meet his family. We all went, and although everyone was very kind and accepting, I didn't feel as if I belonged. I didn't feel I wanted to stay in touch with any of them, and that's okay. This was my life, and no one was going to live it but me. I also have to be comfortable with my own decisions. Overall, I really wanted my bio mom there to get me away from these people. I knew that was not going to happen, and most likely I would never see or speak to her again, since I went to meet Benny against her wishes.

As time passed, Benny tried very hard to stay in touch with me. He called one day and wanted to drive out to Arizona to visit Anthony and me. He explained that he recently bought a new car and wanted to take a road trip. That made sense to me. I thought I might do the same if I had been freed after twenty years in prison. I would want to go anywhere and everywhere I could. With his limited finances and a fresh start in life, Benny wanted to visit one of his daughters. Christina, my half-sister, was the only person I told besides Anthony. Christina is younger than I am, but she is most definitely the more rational of the two of us. She wasn't thrilled about this idea, and neither was her mom. I love my sister's mom. We all have our own issues, but she loves me and is good to us both. She truly accepted me from the very beginning. I can see now why she and my bio mother were best friends growing up before Benny came into their lives.

One evening, very late, I received a phone call from a police station in a state somewhere between Michigan and Arizona. Benny had been pulled over for a DUI and wanted me to bail him out of jail. I knew then and there that this was going to be a very fucked up situation. I rationalized that bailing him out of jail was the least I could do for someone who gave my sister and me life.

Christina and I are very close and share everything, just like sisters should. I certainly hit the jackpot with my siblings. My brothers and sister that are in my life are truly amazing, ambitious, loving humans, and they give me all the love that I could possibly need. They make up for the lack of love from any of my parents. Jackie is the exception from my parents' generation. She has been that pillar of love and strength for me from the moment I was born.

I'm blessed in many ways, and choosing to focus on my blessings seemed to help me turn my compassionate side towards Benny that night. Yes, I bailed him out while he was on his journey to meeting me again. I was grateful that I could help, and that I had an amazing job that allowed me the opportunity to help. I knew I would never see that money again. It became a gift.

Communication, trust, honesty, and basic integrity is required in my eyes in all relationships. Anthony and I were doing worse as every day went by. I was a workaholic and loved it, and he wanted to party while he was getting ready to (barely) graduate from medical school. How he ever graduated with all the partying he did, I will never know.

With the pressure of Benny coming, my job, and Anthony and me living very different lives under one roof, I started to view Anthony more as a roommate than a husband. It was evident that we were growing apart as his jealousy raged and the fights began. I wasn't even attracted to him anymore.

Daily life continued, such as it was, and a few days later Benny arrived. The problem right out of the gate was his lack of honesty. Anthony and I both went to work during the day and Anthony had a lot of classes at night. Benny, being our house guest, could go to the pool, relax, go sight seeing, etcetera. Well, that didn't happen. One day at work I received a phone call from a neighbor who also happened to be one of my best friends. Ginny told me my front door was wide open and my two dogs were running around our community. I shared this bizarre story with my boss, and we both knew something was off. Doug told me to go home and check out the situation.

Having a life, and a very full life at that, we all have personal problems. But, I did not like personal problems in my workplace. I couldn't seem to avoid this, though. When I got to my house I found my dogs running around the street. Fortunately, I got them back into the house and to safety before either one of them got hit by a car, then I walked into the house and found Benny passed out on the floor with the stove on.

I scanned the room and put it all together when I tried to wake up Benny and found a needle sticking out of his arm. That was the moment when I froze. I didn't know what to do. I grabbed Benny and shook him to see if he was alive before I called 911. Benny came to right away, luckily, but he was high as a kite and on heroin.

What kind of person goes to another person's home as a guest, and takes so many drugs that he passes out with the stove on? Oh, I guess I just answered my question. A total loser drug addict, that's who! I took care of Benny that day, and the next morning I took him to a methadone clinic in downtown Phoenix. I was scared and I felt betrayed. I told Benny he couldn't stay with us anymore and had to leave that day. He did not leave easily. He wrote nasty, horrible letters saying that because I kicked him out he was going to kill me and my half-sister Christina. Me first, then drive back to Michigan and murder her. I was so scared that I contacted the police. Benny had left the letters on my car windshield, and I had hung on to them for proof. I also called my sister and read her the letters. In the letters he said he was going to "kill us and spit on our graves because we both didn't want anything to do with him."

After less than a week Benny finally drove himself back to Michigan. I don't know how he got the gas money, but I didn't care who saved his ass as long as he was gone. I was just grateful I wasn't calling my sister everyday and looking out the window reporting to her that he was still sitting or sleeping in his car (which was parked in back of my house) like a crazy stalker.

Neither of us ever spoke to Benny again. My biological father is still a stranger to me, but I didn't sign up for any of his crap. He was a grown man, and bio dad or not, I was not going to be his parent. Nor was I going to take care of him and his drug abuse problems.

The Universe Always Has a Plan

I WAS HANGING OUT at home one evening and it occurred to me that I hadn't heard from Anthony. And as a matter of fact, I didn't even know where he was. I did remember thinking he probably was with friends. Maybe he went out for drinks after work? We hadn't been getting along, and all I could think about was divorce, but I didn't know how I was going to tell him. I had asked him a week previously if we could sit down to discuss our marriage, and he had been avoiding me ever since. This was the night we were supposed to have our talk.

It was approximately two AM when the phone rang. I had fallen asleep hours earlier. I was groggy, but heard Anthony say I needed to pick him up, that there had been a car accident. I also heard sirens in the background, along with the sounds of a few drunk girls giggling.

I reminded Anthony that he was supposed to come home after work so we could talk about our marriage. Then I mentioned since his priorities were so far up his ass, he could get a ride from one of the girls I heard in the background. "And, oh and by the way," I finished. "Since you're not here for me to talk with you in person, I might as well tell you over the phone that I want a divorce!"

I hung up, then left the phone off the hook for the rest of the night. I also locked my master bedroom door. That way when Drunk Ass (my new name for Anthony), got home, he would have to sleep in the guest room or on the sofa—whichever one he could make it to. I had no idea what state he might be in, but in my mind, from that moment on, he was no longer my problem. I had turned off my feelings for him like a light switch without a bulb, and there was no turning me back on. I was one pissed off wife!

I needed to go back to sleep, as I knew the following hours would be more than I had anticipated. With my recent words, I needed all the sleep I could get—especially if Anthony came home and fought with me. It was going to go down one way or another; he would either fight or pass out. I prayed to God that he would pass out on the couch. I prayed until I fell asleep.

The next few days brought the same routine with both of us avoiding each other and only speaking in passing. I was getting my affairs in order for a quick and easy divorce. How hard could it be? I didn't have children with him and I didn't buy real estate with him, so it should be easy. It was an easier split that way. Fifty-fifty. That's Arizona law, and anyhow, it was fair.

Of course he would have to move, because our rental was provided through my job. It was part of my salary. I also helped pay for his medical school. When Anthony and I finally spoke I told him he needed to stay in the guest room until he found a new place to live, and we would just split up everything. That, to me, meant the furniture. I would keep my car and he would keep his truck. While I made decent money for someone my age, we were young and didn't have any savings to speak of. Basically we paid our bills, but lived paycheck to paycheck.

It sounded pretty easy, although hearts were involved and that always has a tendency to make matters that could have been simple into something more malicious in nature. I wanted to play nice with Anthony, but I also wanted my own life. So, I started hanging out with my own friends. I reached out to Joey from work and started spending time with him, and with his roommate Matt, and Matt's girlfriend Jen. The four of us became best friends and we started to spend weekends hanging out, going to shows, dancing, drinking, and shooting pool. We were broke as fuck, but still managed to have fun, get our bills paid, buy food, and we had our own places.

Matt and Joey had a small punk rock hole in the wall that Jen was brave enough to move into with Matt. I crashed with Joey all the time. It was perfect and fun, with only a little drama of the kind sometimes seen between friends. I also started hanging out more with Ginny, my neighbor. We had so much fun that I started staying at her house more than mine.

A few months earlier, Anthony had bought concert tickets for us, and for many of his co-workers and friends who had moved with us from California. We were five to six couples deep, and because I was friends with all of them too, I was convinced that Anthony and I could play nice for one day. We would be at a huge twenty-one and over venue called Club Rio in Tempe, Arizona on January 28, 1996, Super Bowl Sunday. The club was guaranteed to have many, many people, lots of distractions, and a good time! At the very least I was hoping for a great buzz. At best, maybe it would be a way for Anthony and me to part civilly, and to smooth things over between us for an easy break.

Of course, that's not what happened. We hadn't been in the club five minutes before he started being cocky and a jerk. We began to fight right out of the gate. I went straight to the bar to get a drink, and a guy came up to me. He asked if I wouldn't mind watching his band play; they were coming on next. I told him I was waiting for my drink, and that I had many people with me; we had just gotten here.

Turned out the guy was the lead singer of the band. I've tried, but for the life of me can't remember the band's name. They were opening up on one of the side stages and had plenty of room for people to watch them. It would mean the world to him if I was there.

I got it. Either the guy thought I was cute or he needed to draw a larger crowd. Maybe it was both. Who knows? Regardless, I found seats up front and I have to admit, I couldn't stand the heat in Arizona. I was miserably hot, and these were the perfect seats to get out of the heat, have a drink or two, and get into the concert vibe. Anthony and his friends found me and we sat down to watch one of the worst bands I've ever seen. Anthony was being loud and a dick, and finally took off with some of his guy friends. Everyone began to spread out, so I decided to use the restroom and get another drink.

I discovered that our friends had left me alone, but I didn't care. I was perfectly happy being alone, so I paid for my drink and headed back outside where the seats were, and sat right in front of the fountain, center stage. The next band that came on was a band I'd never seen before but they were pretty well-known to the locals, apparently, and the crowd started filling up the seats. I decided to enjoy my cocktail, and besides, I wanted to see what this unique set of rocker-light characters had to bring.

Normally I went to punk shows and this was more of a radio station type of festival. This was a much larger crowd and a much larger venue than I was used to—and so much to look at. Even if the next band wasn't good, I was being entertained by all the other people who were watching. The next band that came on had a singer who was tall and skinny, with tattoos and skinny little dreadlocks that fell just past his shoulders.

As the band started to play I realized they were really good. The singer's voice was amazing, but I found it odd that while he was singing he stared right at me. Almost the entire time, every song he sang, it was as if he was singing directly to me. I thought his girl-friend or wife must be behind me, because I'd never seen this person before in my life.

I turned around to see if there was someone behind me who he was staring at. Then a girl sitting to my left asked if *I* was his girl-friend. I said no, but then other people came up asking the same thing. It was all very strange, but it made me start to pay closer at-tention to the band. Members who stood out to me were the bassist and the vocalist. They were pretty much the show. As the set pro-gressed, quite a bit of synergy developed between the singer and me, to the point that this wasn't just a concert anymore. It had be-come a spiritual connection.

After the band finished, they went behind the stage, but there was a side area where I could see them. I stayed in my seat, drinking my drink and talking to a girl named Penny who was depressed. She was so sad she started to cry. I told her I was in the middle of a di-vorce and that she should enjoy her time, enjoy being in the mo-ment. She seemed like she needed support, so I extended my friendship.

The next band was getting ready to come on and their roadies were setting up their gear. The boyfriend of one of my on-site prop-erty managers, Amy, was one of the roadies, and he recognized me. "Hey," he said. "There's my girlfriends boss, Sam. Let's bring her backstage."

It was nice to see a friendly face. He asked who I was with and I filled him in on the drama with Anthony. Everyone from work knew about Anthony, but no one there had ever met him. He asked if I wanted to hang with them backstage, so I asked if Penny could join me. It's always easier to bring a few girls backstage than a whole crew of people. Plus, I knew I would be harder to find and would be safe from Anthony. Before we got there, he and I had decided that we weren't leaving until the very end. I had hours, and was going to have fun no matter what.

So, Penny and I went backstage. Right away we ran into two members of the band that had just played: the guitar player and the drummer. They offered me a CD, and asked if I liked their show. I told everyone I was with to buy a CD. Even then I knew it was important to support our local bands and music scene. All of us bought their CD that night, including Anthony. They both also invited me to see them play at their next gig. They went on to say they were just about to sign a record deal.

As we were talking, I saw the singer sitting down on a barstool in the back, so I went up to him to introduce myself. This is when Samantha Olit and Chester Bennington first met. We started talking and were getting along extremely well. Turned out the poor guy was super sick with a temperature of 103 degrees. He also wore glasses that he did not wear when he was performing. I guessed it would be pretty hard to wear glasses while he was jumping all over the stage. His voice was completely captivating, and his energy level was insane. You would never have known that he was sick.

Soon, we started to get into a deep conversation. He told me he was twenty-one and I told him I was twenty-two, actually, twenty-three in December. He said he would be twenty-two in March, so I was a bit older. Right away, we started to share our life stories.

Penny came over, drunk now, and started to hang all over the lead singer. She was annoying, but I was sure he dealt with that all the time. After all, his band, Grey Daze, was the number one local band in Phoenix and had a very strong following. Just before the singer and I could exchange phone numbers, a bouncer walked up to him and for reasons I didn't understand then, the bouncer chased him out. I then became distracted by Anthony and his friends, who found me. Anthony started hanging on me, drunk, and I was trying to keep the peace.

After we got home, I stayed up all night thinking about the spiritual connection I had developed with the stranger I had met, the one who sang to me and stared into my eyes for a good forty-five minutes. I couldn't explain it. While I was listening to the CD I was looking at it and never noticed that, on the back, was their manager's phone number in plain view so anyone could contact them. I was mesmerized by the encounter and laid there wondering if I would ever meet the man again.

The next morning all I could think about was the cute guy I had met at the concert. I was a little bouncier than usual, which was saying a lot. I'm always pretty bouncy, but today was different. I felt for the first time that someone saw my soul, and that I had seen his. I didn't realize that not only did I feel differently, but my feelings showed to everyone who interacted with me.

My co-workers started to ask questions about Super Bowl weekend and the concert at Club Rio. How did I like the club? How was Anthony's behavior? What bands played? They kept pushing for info, and gave me a hard time in a fun and caring way. My co-workers pushed and teased me all morning; they didn't even care if I did my job that day. Of course I had to work, but everyone was enjoying meddling in my love life.

Funny thing, at the beginning of my divorce, love was the part of my life that I had sworn off for eternity. I said things such as, "I'm never going to get married again, just get me through this damn divorce and I will stay single forever." Or, "I'm going to be single and play the field. I never want a boyfriend ever again." I meant every word I said.

After all my swearing off relationships for life, I was more serious than I have ever been. Who was I kidding? The universe had to throw a wrench into my plans and have a tall, skinny, dreadlocked, bad dressing, broke ass musician sing to me and capture my attention. Now I couldn't even focus on my work! That morning my entire staff surrounded my desk wanting to know the details of every moment. Most of my co-workers were married, so they were living vicariously through me.

I told the amazing story of how I had a spiritual, but difficult to explain, experience. After I had answered every question, one co worker said, "Why don't you look him up, as if you were looking for a "for sale by owner?" That was a real estate term for trying to get new listings and future business.

"Are you insane?" I asked.

As if I would do any of that. No way! But, the entire office teamed up on me. They pushed all day until I looked up every Bennington in the phone book and had called every one, trying to reach the stranger I had met the night before.

Everyone in the office stood around my desk, sat on the corner of my desk, or paced back and forth waiting with anticipation to see if the tactic would work. I was trembling with fear. I was so afraid I wouldn't find him, but on the other hand I thought, "what if I did?" I also didn't want him to think I was a stalker.

It's funny, because I didn't want to be in a relationship. I wanted a divorce and was in the middle of one. The possibility of starting something new went against everything I thought I wanted. I was more afraid of not trying, though, because it was clear that the universe and God were playing a huge roll in this, and they had gi-normous plans for Chester and me.

In reality, I was more afraid of not seeing him again than I was to call around to try to find him. Thank goodness for my loving and pushy co-workers. Honestly, I wouldn't have done it without all of them pushing me in the right direction.

It was around three o'clock in the afternoon, or maybe three-thirty, when a woman answered my call. Her voice sounded young and sweet, and she gave me an opportunity to share my story, tell her why I was calling.

"My name is Samantha," I said, "and I know this is going to sound weird. However, last night at a show I met a guy who might be your brother. He probably meets tons of people all the time, but I want you to know I'm not a crazy stalker chick. So in the event he remembers me, can you please give him my name and number? I promise I will not contact you again. But, if he wants to contact me, the ball is now in his court."

Turned out the woman's name was Renee and she was his older sister. She said the man I was searching for was indeed her brother. She continued to explain that while usually she did not reveal any info about her brother, for some odd reason she decided to tell me. If that's not the universe or God intervening, then I don't know what is!

I thanked his sister for her understanding, and for passing on my information. It was nice to speak with her and I was at peace because at least I tried. I took action with pure intention and in recognition of the life opportunity that was presented to me. I really just followed my heart, but was, in fact, manifesting the life I wanted.

I wanted a divorce, but my desire to be in a marriage full of passion, and live with true love, must have been stronger. My will to *love* is a pure emotion that drives all my decision making.

The next morning, I woke up late for work. I had slept incredibly well, probably because I had so many things off my mind. Anthony had moved into the guest room and I had found a new roommate. Gabi and I had met in real estate school and as soon as Anthony moved out, Gabi would take over the guest room. As of now, she was sharing the master bedroom with me because I wasn't comfortable living alone with Anthony anymore. Unfortunately, Anthony had become an angry young man.

I rushed into work and had much catching up to do from not

working much the day before. Pissing off my boss was not an option, nor was losing my job. I adored and respected my boss and was grateful to him for many things.

When I got there the office was in high vibration, and everyone was in catch-up mode. There was some radical energy going on, and everyone closed deals that day. We were so busy that I forgot all about the day before and trying to find the man of my dreams. But in the middle of all the business and hustle the phone rang . . . and I answered it.

"Hello," a man said. "Is Samantha there?"

My whole world stopped. It was *him*!

"This is she," I said.

The office got quiet and I couldn't hear anything but his voice. He said how excited he was to hear from me and had been so surprised when his sister called the night before. He worked late nights at Burger King at the drive through window, which helped pay his bills between shows with his band. This job also gave him flexibility, with days off to play gigs.

I had left my work number with his sister thinking it was safer than a home number. After all, he was still a stranger and this was all very new. Chester again said how happy he was to hear from me, and from that day on I received a phone call from him every morning, noon, and night for two weeks until I finally agreed to meet him. We could have met earlier, but I was trying to bring my relationship with Anthony to a clean end before jumping into something new. During our evening calls, Chester and I stayed on the phone for hours.

I finally went to see his band play one evening with Gabi and Anthony. Anthony insisted on dropping us off, saying he would be our designated driver. What in the world was I thinking? I didn't want Anthony to drop me off anywhere, but I also didn't want to fight over anything either.

It was completely awkward, all of us being in the same place together. Chester and I had spent the last two weeks discussing everything about each other's personal lives, and getting to know each other. After the show we all got drinks and Gabi and the guitar player started to flirt and were hitting it off. Everyone was in great conversation, and there was a love connection going on in more than one way. Chester was sitting next to me and was playing footsie with me under the table. Everyone that evening could feel the chemistry between us, and that didn't go over well with Anthony—even though we were legally separated and were trying to maintain a friendship.

On the way home, Gabi talked the entire time about her new crush, which was a perfect distraction. I didn't want to have to answer, explain, or communicate with Anthony about anything. I could listen to Gabi, I could sing to the radio, and I could have been just buzzed enough to walk into the house, go upstairs, and B-line it to my bedroom. Nighty night. Whew, I made it! Time to pass out.

That evening Chester had asked me out for a dinner date for the upcoming Friday. He had asked me to his apartment and I went to his place after I got off work. When I arrived, his roommate and Grey Daze guitar player, Bobby, answered the door and we exchanged hellos and hugs as he invited me in. I looked around to find Chester in overalls painting on a couch that was outside on the balcony. He was a very interesting artist who loved to paint and share his art.

After he was finished with his painting, we went inside and decided to go to the store. He wanted to cook me dinner and I thought that was pretty romantic. I loved that we went grocery shopping together on our first date. We were silly, walking around the store, going up and down the isles, trying to find the ingredients for a salad, spaghetti, and homemade garlic bread. A simple, easy dinner, yet it was barely in his budget. I do not think he had two pennies to rub together at that time. So, I pitched in because I had noticed he was low on the basics around the house. If I was going to be there, I needed a few comforts as well.

We got all the ingredients for our dinner, including our adult beverages: a bottle of wine, some beer, and a bottle of Jack. I helped him buy laundry detergent, toothpaste, and most important, toilet paper! We had so much fun shopping together, cooking, and spending time with one another. It really gave us a chance to know one another. You don't have to have a lot of money to achieve a romantic evening.

This, by far, was turning into one of the most fun and interesting dates I'd ever had. Chester started to cook, and we had drinks, great conversation, and listened to all kinds of music. His roommate, Bobby, also joined us. I had such a great time with Bobby and Chester. It was fun getting to know them both, and Chester and I had all night to have quality alone time. Chester and I both gravitated to reggae music, as it was our mutual favorite. He was impressed by my knowledge and we quickly realized how compatible we were. The more time that went by the more we discovered about each other.

The dinner he made was amazing. I don't know if it tasted better than most of my dinners because he was a very good cook, or if it was due to the adventure of it all and having a guy I was totally into cook me dinner. The dinner was definitely made with love and we had all the typical sparks of young love. It was one of my all time favorite traditional Italian dinners I had ever eaten, even though we were young and poor. Both of us lived paycheck to paycheck and we both had roommates. That was part of the fun, having friends to hang with, share adventures with, and save money by sharing expenses so we could do all the grown up things and have an amazing time doing them.

After dinner the three of us played Jenga®. It's a fun game of skill where players take turns removing one block at a time from a tower. We drank, laughed, and finished our drinks, then Chester and I decided to call it a night. I hadn't been planning to stay the night, but after several cocktails and a hot-n-heavy make out session, he talked me into it.

The next morning, I got up and was rushing to get home so I could get ready and get my ass to work. When we woke up he confessed that he "sort of" had a girlfriend, but they had broken up because she was messed up on heroin. WTF? I gave him a kiss on his forehead, collected my things, and without saying anything, I bounced out in a hurry. I got to my car and I heard Chester screaming, "Sam, wait. Wait a minute."

I got into my car, and rolled down the window as he tried to talk his way out of what he had just shared with me.

"I have to get to work and don't want to be late," I said. And that was that. I drove away but pulled over a few blocks later and balled my bloody eyes out. Wow, this was certainly a dirty trick God was playing on me.

Chester called as usual, but I didn't answer. He kept calling and I still didn't answer. I was heartbroken and didn't want to waste time on a guy who may or may not have a girlfriend. And, she was on drugs (according to him) and that scared the shit out of me. Also, if he had a girlfriend, I did not want to be second choice. I'm not a home wrecker. I have a rule that I never will be the "other" woman.

I was in the middle of a divorce and was keeping all my personal drama under wraps. After many months, Anthony and I were at the point where we would not see each other for days. I was just waiting for him to hit his breaking point and move in with a friend or co-worker.

A few days later, Gabi had plans to go out with Bobby for drinks. I'm pretty sure it was a date. They invited me to go but I didn't want to be a third wheel. But, both of them begged me to go. Maybe, Gabi was afraid to be alone and needed a wingman? I finally decided, why not? I wanted to go out but thought I'd better look good in case I ran into Chester.

That evening Bobby picked us up and brought us to the Electric Ballroom. That was a local spot where their band played frequently. We got some drinks and headed over to play some pool. I didn't see Chester right away, but as I stood near the pool table getting ready to play our first round, I spotted him in a dark corner, waiting for his moment to confront me. When he did, he backed me up against a table and kissed me. He kissed me so much that I couldn't talk or even breathe. I soon changed my mind about not dating him.

According to what Bobby and Gabi shared with me, the moment Chester opened his big mouth about the girlfriend/ex-girlfriend, he said, "that was the biggest mistake of my life." Chester added that he was sure he wanted to be with me. That was the night we officially became a couple.

From then on we rarely were apart, except for work and the occasional night I decided to go home. We always stayed at his place because Anthony was still at mine. Anthony was becoming more aggressive, and Chester and Bobby didn't want me staying there anymore. They were both becoming more and more concerned for my safety.

7

Love Conquers Challenges

ONE DAY CHESTER CALLED me at work to ask if I would join him on a long weekend in Mexico to visit some of his friends. We were newly dating, I didn't know any of his friends, and was a bit afraid to go out of the country with people I barely knew. But, I decided to go after all, and felt safe because I was with Chester. His friends headed down the day before we did, because we both had to work. We decided to leave right after work and I think we both got off a little early, as we had both pleaded with our bosses all day.

Growing up in California I had many opportunities to go Mexico, but was afraid to go because I had been told stories of how you can be kidnapped or robbed, that traveling as a young lady can be dangerous. But, I was excited to get to Rocky Point, Mexico. We stayed at Plaza La Marina Paseo las Glorias, a fun spring break spot very close to Arizona. Our drive down was the craziest and the greatest road trip ever. The things you can do while driving a car and not crash! So fun. We were wild, young, and free.

After our first romantic get away, one that was as romantic as two kids could get who live paycheck-to-paycheck, we confirmed that Chester was going to give notice at his apartment and move in with me. We were always together, so why should we pay for two separate places? As soon as my divorce was final, I would purchase my townhome. This made sense to us both; we were madly in love.

After our wonderful weekend, we went back to the grind, and that next Monday morning was busy at work, as usual. The phone rang, and it was my bestie and favorite neighbor ever, Ginny. Ginny suggested I get home as soon as possible because Anthony was moving out—but things didn't look right to her. My dogs (Bandit, an Akita, and Tashi, an Australian Shepard rescue) were going crazy, as there were people they hadn't seen before in my house.

I knew Anthony well and trusted that he would never be too below the belt. We had loved each other very much at one point, right? It's so weird how you can love someone so much, and then one day not love them anymore. Anyway, over time, we (maybe just me) grew apart. I wanted more and so did he, but I wanted more without him, and he knew that in his heart of hearts.

I left work and got home to find he had taken the ironing board but left the iron, took the coffee pot but left the machine. I think you get the picture. He did this throughout the house, which made me crazy mad. I yelled at him in the middle of the street and even kicked his stupid truck as he drove off. The worst part was that I hurt my foot more than I hurt him or his ego. Anthony and I never saw each other again, and we have not spoken since.

For our divorce hearing, Anthony did not show up in court. But, our divorce was granted anyway and our marriage finally was over. He kept his car and I kept mine. We left our marriage and went our separate ways: he with a degree and a future career, and I with my career. Looking back, our marriage was an immature move for us both, but we were both big risk takers and wanted more than our lives provided at the time. For us both to grow we had to put ourselves out of our comfort zone and push through adversity. That way we could grow and find out who we were. When people are young, I always tell them to go for it. Make your dreams come true and risk it while you are not locked into a family—and while you have the freedom to take risks to succeed. I looked at my relationship with Anthony as pushing each other to grow, and then we each moved on with our lives.

♥

While Anthony was absent for the end of our marriage, Chester went with me to the divorce hearing. He was extremely supportive and we were on the fast track of building our brand new lives together. We were now living together and Gabi was our roommate. Oddly enough, Chester used to have nightmares about her killing me. He had these nightmares all the time. In fact, he was so freaked out that she was going to hurt me that he made me ask her to move out.

When I told Gabi the news, at first she was like, over a guy? Really? Bro's before ho's, and that expression goes both ways. This was different. I tried to explain to her how in love we were and I was putting my priorities into my relationship with him. A true friend would want to see me happy. I had zero intention of hurting her, but my life was changing. It made sense that eventually she would move out, because Chester and I had just moved in together.

It's important if you have roommates that everyone lives in a harmonious environment. The only way it could be harmonious was if Gabi moved out—in Chester's opinion. I trusted him, but unfortunately it was the end of my friendship with her. As I have grown in life, I have realized that some people are in my life for minutes, some for days, some for weeks, months, decades, and then there are the lifers. I already knew that Chester was going to be my husband, so if he was uncomfortable with Gabi living with us, she had to go.

One evening at the Electric Ball Room, Chester had a show and all of his friends and family, and even his ex-girlfriend were there. She had grown up with the same people Chester had. I wasn't thrilled that she was there, but I wasn't threatened either. My friends were there, too. The place was packed and he and his band were opening for the nineties band Seven Mary Three, best known for the song, "Cumbersome." We were watching the show, drinking, dancing, and having a blast when Chester started to sing "Anything Anything" by Dramarama. The song had a repetitive "marry me, marry me" lyric. His best friends Mark, Donnie, and Jason, turned me around and pushed me to the front of the stage. Mark yelled in my ear, "Pay attention. Chester is asking you to marry him in front of everyone." OMG! I had no clue! I just thought he was singing another cover song.

As I gave Chester my attention, he sang to me and asked me to marry him.

"Yes," I said. Then I started to cry.

I was so happy and in shock! I just wasn't expecting that at all. He caught me by surprise and it was so perfect to have so many friends and family there to share that moment. It became a night of celebration over and beyond the normal evening of a kick ass show.

Later that night, at home, he asked me to marry him again. He even got down on one knee, and of course I started to cry all over again. We were so happy, and so crazy in love with one another.

We were house poor, but were not going to let that get in the way of our love, or our life plans. We decided to tattoo our wedding bands, and as a gift from Derek, a friend and artist who we both loved dearly, he tattooed us as our wedding present. The gift had double the meaning to us both, because he was one of our closest friends.

We also had to borrow money so we could get plain wedding bands for each other. My adopted grandmother had passed away and I inherited her engagement ring with diamonds and emeralds, so I used those stones for my wedding ring. I like to have meaningful intentions in the things I possess or hold dear to my heart, and that ring was, and is, very special to me.

This was March of 1996 and Chester and I set a wedding date for October 31 of that year. Our favorite holiday was Halloween, and the idea of wearing all black on my wedding day was cool and edgy. I was married before, so I didn't want to wear white—although white is one of my favorite colors. We also wanted a classy, traditional wedding, but done our way.

Late one afternoon some of Chester's closest friends came to the house to hang, and I heard Donnie say, "Dude, you have to tell her!" Donnie said this a few times.

"Dude, I will!" Chester said, but I heard the stress in his voice.

As I passed by, I said, "Tell me what?" My first instinct was that he had a horrible disease, and I felt my thoughts spiraling down the rabbit hole.

When Chester finally spoke, he said, "When we first met at the concert, I said I was twenty-one. Remember? It was a twenty-one and older show?"

"Yes, I remember," I said. As a reminder, we met when I was twenty-two. I had turned twenty-two in December 1995 and we met in January 1996. The next December I would be twenty-three.

"Well," he said. "I'm not twenty-one. I'm twenty."

That was a bit of a shock, but then I saw Donnie cross his arms in disapproval.

"Okay," Chester said. "I'm not twenty, I'm really nineteen."

That's when I about spit out my water. I felt like, "Stop! Do not tell me if you're any younger." Chester thought I was going to call off the wedding and started to panic. While Donnie calmed him down, I sat there in shock. I needed a moment to process the news. I was so upset that he had lied to me, but I also still loved him very much. Now the reason the bouncer threw Chester out of the club the night we met made sense. Chester was underage. He could be there to perform, but after, he had to leave. It was a lot to take in, as age matters more when you are young.

All that kept running through my mind, though, was how much in love I was with Chester. Age didn't matter—as long as we were both legal! That was a big deal to me. The wedding would go on, partly due to Chester's father and his wife at the time, who helped us plan and who helped financially with the wedding. We were both so incredibly grateful, especially because we didn't have a pot to piss in. We didn't have much money, but all that mattered was that we were happy!

♥

Four months before our wedding we found out that Chester might have fathered a child born to his ex-girlfriend from high school. My explanation here is from my perspective, and probably like yours, my perspective is constantly learning, evolving, and being the best I can be with integrity. Chester's ex-girlfriend had a perspective. And, Chester had a perspective, too. Somewhere in the middle of the various perspectives of three young adults lies the truth.

Truth be told, we all handled the situation very poorly out of fear, immaturity, and poverty. No matter what, children are a blessing. As you can imagine, this is a very strong emotion for me since I am adopted.

The mother, potential father, and the bride to be (me), all handled things the best we knew how—but we didn't know the perspective of others who were involved. I quickly understood, though, that as the young father, Chester had a very different set of fears than the mother. As the new bride standing on the outside, but living very much on the inside, I had my own thoughts and feelings. Yes,

I definitely had my own challenges while also dealing with other people's decisions and feelings.

In general, people learn lessons in the future, after they have already experienced a challenge. But, I had to learn my lessons here as I went, and I do not think I learned very well in the moment in this particular situation. We all were so very young.

Looking back, this was the beginning of my awakening. This is where I first became truly aware. Even though I was young, due to my spiritual beliefs and my self-teachings from the age of seven through trauma with my adopted mother, I was now awakening and becoming more aware every day. When a person is this young and experiences raising his or her vibration to protect from being an extreme empath, it forces some, like me, to become extremely independent and strong. Empaths have the ability to pick up on other people's mental or emotional states in an intuitive way.

I do wish I could have stayed a kid a while longer. Adulting is hard! There was not a single person in my world whom I could speak to about my awakening and growth through these difficult times. The events happening in these times were also out of my control.

I did realize that everyone involved had different choices to make and the choices were going to be a challenge for all of us. Just so you know, I have intentionally left out details of this part of my story. Some of you might remember this time in our lives and wonder why I have not gone into details or explained my perspective in more depth. I have a good reason, and it's simple. This is my story. Although I have touched on many important factors in my life, the bottom line is that this particular event is really not "my" story. This story belongs to the mother, father, and child. If I felt the need to defend my position as a woman, mother, wife, or step-mother, then I certainly would. However, I have so much more I would like to share that is 100 percent my life, my choice, and my story, that it's more respectful to those involved if I keep it short here.

As a recap: Chester and I met. Two weeks later we started dating, and we soon had our first vacation together. Two months after we met, we were living together. I then got a divorce from Anthony, Chester and I got engaged, we found out my new fiancé may or may not be a father, and nine months after we met, we would become husband and wife.

Chester and I undeniably were becoming a force together. We obviously could handle a lot more than most—even as individuals. But in my eyes, going through life with my soul mate made all of our challenges and dreams so much richer. When you know you just know! We were a solid couple and that was exactly what I wanted with my future husband. He and I were one unit, but we remained true to ourselves while we maintained our individuality. That was when I knew I really and truly was going to marry this man. Sure, there were major red flags, but the love we had for each other fully conquered our fears, and we were on our way to building and creating an exciting new chapter in our lives together.

Love Note

Dear Anthony,

I want you to know that I did love you very much. We were high school sweethearts—at least that was the age we were when we first started dating. We were teenagers, and even though we didn't go to the same high school, you will always be my high school sweetheart.

I know things didn't work out the way either of us had hoped it would, but I am very grateful for the time we spent together. I feel we did a lot of growing up and soul searching during our time together.

I'm proud of you for finishing med school. I'm glad I was part of that journey and that we were in each others lives then. We each were making career moves so we could have a future. We were young and reckless, and no one thought we should have gotten married. Looking back, I agree. Our family and friends were right. We were just too damn young. Thank you for being brave and moving to Arizona for your medical education. If it wasn't for your career move, I would have never have moved there and met my son's father. And, I wouldn't have had my son. So many things wouldn't have taken place if you and I didn't end up in Arizona. I do understand that there is a purpose for us all.

I haven't seen you since the day you moved out of our house. No matter what the court says, that day was the true end of our marriage. I heard through the grapevine, many years later, that you were living with a woman, had a beautiful little boy, and that you passed away at a very young age. I do not know what happened, but I heard your girlfriend was in the shower and that she heard gun shots. I do not know if they ever caught the guys who did this horrific act, and I do not know if they were robbers, or what was going on. I do know that when I heard the news I reached out to your mom right away.

Over the years I have stayed in touch with your mom, sister, and brother. Your siblings are all grown up and are very sweet. Your mom still looks the same and is one of the kindest people I have ever had the privilege to know. She seems happy, although I know a piece of her died when you left this world. Thank God for social media, because I can keep in touch with her and see so many beautiful photos of your family. I even got the chance to see pictures of your beautiful baby boy.

I also stay in touch with several of our childhood friends, especially, Jean, the other Anthony, and David. All are doing very well and our friendships, memories, and stories keep you very much alive. They miss you and will always love you. I know this.

I wish I had a chance to tell you all this in person, and I want you to know that I have no regrets. I was so proud to be your wife, even though we didn't . . . make it last forever.

Love always,
Sam

Creation of a Global Impact

ONE EVENING IN MAY or June, Chester and I went to dinner with my dad and the stepmonster in South Bay. That was the night we were going to share the news of our upcoming wedding. Everyone else knew, but I was afraid of what my dad might say. I wanted his approval, but I also always danced to my own song. At the end of the day, I did what I wanted, no matter if he liked it or not. Certainly, I was a pain in his ass and often pissed him off. I'm older now and was hopeful we could repair and build on our relationship and become close again. After all, my dad was one of the most important people in my life, even if he didn't know it, or didn't care, or feel the same. He just was that important to me.

Chester wanted to tell my dad himself, as he liked and respected my father. He was so excited to be his son-in-law. As the evening progressed I became more nervous by the minute. Finally, just as my dad bit into a piece of shrimp, I blurted it out. "Dad, Chester asked me to marry him and I said yes!"

What was I thinking? I will tell you what I was thinking, I was thinking if his mouth was full and he was going to get angry, he would have to chew first, which gave us all a minute for him to think before he reacted. I thought it was a great plan, but that's not exactly how it played out. Instead, my dad started to choke on his food. I wasn't sure if he needed the Heimlich maneuver or not. Seriously, I was so scared and Chester was ready to kill me! I wasn't trying to kill my dad; I just didn't think it through all the way. Oops!

After a time, my dad collected his composure, had some water, and up went his eyebrows. Fathers always have a way of putting the fear of life into you. Geez, all it took was a raised eyebrow and I started to scramble. I knew my dad liked Chester, but he wanted to know if Chester was going to be able to take care of me, or if he was going to be chasing dreams forever? We both understood that from a father's point of view that this was, and is, a normal reaction. My dad proceeded to ask Chester how he was going to keep me in the lifestyle I had been raised in. Chester had dreadlocks and tattoos, and was a singer for a local rock band—not exactly what a father wants for his baby girl. A struggling musician with no real college background. What were the odds of him truly making it?

The evening ended with a bit of disapproval along with an "I love you," from my dad. That was followed by some hugs and kisses, and then a "See you soon." I'm sure my stepmonster loved that I delivered heavy news to my dad. In her eyes, probably, it was just like me to make it seem like I was dropping a bomb instead of understanding that I was making a life choice that made me happy.

♥

Chester and I decided to get married in a little chapel in Mesa, Arizona and have our reception at the Phoenix Marriott Resort Tempe at The Buttes in Tempe. The two towns were both in the greater Phoenix area, and were only a few miles apart. President Bush was in town on our wedding day, and his visit created a lot of traffic.

Chester was freaking out that he would be late for our wedding, due to the insane amount of traffic. The President of the United States actually caused all of Phoenix to be backed up. Turned out we were all late and Chester got there before I did, so it worked out perfectly. In our mutual lateness, we were all exactly on time.

I cried during the ceremony. There was no way I could control my tears. They were happy tears, but wow, was I overcome by emotion! That was the happiest day of my life because I felt like I was building a family with someone who brought me more happiness than I had ever known. That meant the world to me.

Before I married Chester, I had not felt a strong family bond. I had always felt like the black sheep in my adopted family. Now, I felt I was marrying my soul/life partner and we were going to build a wonderful life together. It really felt as if the two of us were united as one—along with so many wonderful friends who had grown up with each of us as childhood friends. We both had a solid foundation in our friends. I was blessed because I truly loved his friends like brothers, and I had my own separate friendship with every one of them. The love and support we both felt on the day of our wedding fulfilled us and showered us with love and acceptance.

Me being adopted meant that I did not believe certain people really loved me. It is a serious abandonment issue that I struggle with to this day, even though I have met my birth parents and know the unusual circumstances surrounding my birth. The idea of feeling showered with love was bold, because until this point in my life, I never believed anyone loved me.

Without meaning to offend anyone, the reason I cried so much at our wedding was due to the overwhelming feeling of being loved. I do believe that on that day, everyone who was there, no matter if they thought we were young and making a mistake or not, felt the love in the room. I saw their eyes and smiles, and as an extreme empath, I felt their feelings, which added to the overwhelming feeling of love. Thank you to everyone who was there for sharing all the energy and love with us. I truly love you all.

Not all of my family or friends could be at the wedding, and this was for several reasons. One was that our wedding wasn't in California, so that made it hard for my family and friends to attend. Some could not take time off from work or didn't have the money to travel. My dad didn't make it, nor did my little brothers, who were too young to travel without their parents. Actually, no one from California came—except for my adopted mom. My adoptive mom, by the way, adored Chester. He never got frazzled, and was the calm that settled between us when my mother lashed out verbally, as she sometimes did. I was so glad she could share this very special moment in my life.

Chester and I understood. Well, we tried to understand, but selfishly, I wanted them all there. I'm not 100 percent sure either of us completely understood my dad not being there, however, everyone else had a hall pass and were all very present in our life.

With long-distance blessings from my bio mom, and Scotty and Celine, that was all I needed. That mattered the most, because those two counted! I also had friends from Arizona there, and that was special because these were friends I met before I met Chester. It was as if I lived in two different worlds. One was in California, and the other was my Arizona home. It was important to me to have a little of my own support, but again, I was so blessed with his friends and family who accepted me. Over the coming years, every one of those people would become a close friend or family. It was Arizona meets California, and we became a very large melting pot.

As a married couple, we didn't want to be in debt, so instead of a large wedding, we decided to buy a house and put our honeymoon on pause. This was my second wedding so I didn't hope or expect my dad to help pitch in, and he didn't. He had already done that for my wedding to Anthony. Clearly, I was on my own.

We both had big dreams, and I believed that together we would make both his dreams and mine come true. So, we decided to rent out the condo I bought before we were married and buy a semi-custom home in Paradise Valley, Arizona to move into after the wedding. I loved real estate and learning every avenue of the industry was interesting to me. Some areas of real estate I gravitated to more than others, and sometimes I'd switch to a higher paying job and suck it up so Chester could focus on his God given talent.

A while back I had left my job with Doug. Change is good and I was not able to grow any further with that company. My life with Chester consisted of late nights both during the week and on weekends. He always had either band practice or a show, so I needed more free evenings. It was time to switch my stepping stones to success to ensure the bills were paid so Chester could focus on his music.

That voice! Chester had a talent and a voice the world needed to hear. I knew that with all of my soul, and I absolutely loved his band. I loved the rock vibe and the way he wrote songs. His lyrics always moved my soul. I believed in my husband with every ounce of my being, and I trusted in him, my best friend.

I knew without any doubt that Chester would make it in the music industry. Even when he didn't believe in himself, I believed in him. I can't explain it, but I knew he was going to make his dreams come true. And, when Chester made his dreams come true, with us making that happen together, sacrificing everything and taking enormous risks, even though it was scary at times, through that, I knew all my dreams would come true as well. When Chester didn't believe and was ready to give up, it didn't matter, because I was there to pick him up, keep the home front steady, and the bills paid. I *believed*, and my intuition just knew.

Always, I had seen flashes of a story, like a short film or scene, in my head. I call them flashes, but most call them visions. I was more in sync with my visions now, as they had grown stronger and clearer than when I was younger. It seemed the older I became, the better I understood my feelings, emotions, visions, and belief system. Really, it all came down to how people, things, and events made me feel.

There were people in the industry who were really into Chester's voice, and over the years, I was fortunate to become friends with many of them. I learned from my a.k.a. mom Jackie to invest in family, friends, and business. She taught me right, and her teachings and words of kindness and wisdom rang true to my heart. I can only build on relationships if they're genuine and make me feel good, and so many people loved Chester's voice, I often said, "anyone who is smart or can hear with their ears will fall in love with his voice!" I knew I wasn't being biased.

As his local band heard all the buzz and people in the industry began to rave over this new, talented young voice, the one and only mistake I saw the band make was not including Chester in any business decisions. The band was not forthcoming, and in my opinion, it was from fear that if Chester knew how much industry folks loved his voice and wanted to sign him, he would leave. But, Chester was loyal and loved making music with his bandmates. I believe he would have preferred to grow with them than to break up with them.

But, the band did not stay together anyway. What ultimately broke up the band and drove Chester away was the fact that they did not include him in business decisions. If they couldn't trust him, he certainly could not trust them. He discussed this with them several times and expressed his concern and desire to be more involved. Chester was the youngest member and they always treated him like a dumb, young kid, but he was the one with the huge vocal pipes! Big mistake on their part, and I bet they still regret their choice.

Chester dreamt his entire life of being a lead vocalist, performing on stage for millions. He was determined at a very young age, and even stole his first microphone out of a church, for God sakes! No pun intended. I believe God/Source wanted him to have the microphone, or he would have been busted for theft. I believe it was meant for him because it was all so effortless, the way he found the microphone, or did the microphone find him? I love this story to my core, and never got tired of hearing it from him or one of his childhood friends. No matter what was in our future, with Chester's God given gift of angelic vocal chords, our passion, our determination, and with me by his side, I knew we were going to succeed. I also supported my husband in every way: emotionally, physically, and financially.

I came home from work one day to find no one home. That was weird. I walked around the house saying, "Hello? Is anyone home?" I walked around the entire house thinking maybe Chester was in the garage or the backyard.

Then Chester and his dad walked in. Chester gave me a kiss and said, "Okay, honey. I'm going with Pops to get all my equipment from the practice studio. Oh, and by the way, I just quit the band. Be home straight after!"

My heart sank and I was in a bit of shock. I loved his band. I loved the music they made, but most important, I loved my husband. His happiness meant more to me than any band.

I also was very much in the know and couldn't argue with why he decided to leave, or why he choose to have his father go with him to the studio. Chester brought his father to insure he could get in and out with his equipment without a blow up or physical fight. He should have been treated as an equal and a man, even if he was younger. So, if the other band members were not going to include him in business matters, then Chester was out and that was final.

Pops and Chester did just as they said, and headed to the studio, which was in the garage of one of the band members. Father and son loaded up all the new equipment, and then both were home in time for dinner. I was still in shock and that tripped Chester out a bit. But, I was always supportive. However, I was calculating in my head what would be the best next move for my husband, and how could I help. When I'm quiet and in deep thought it scares people, because I normally have a lot to say, so when I become silent it's either because of deep thought or I'm pissed off, and the pissed off part is what he was worried about.

I wasn't mad at Chester. I was just concerned. To be honest, I was mad at the band. They hurt my husband's feelings, and when he hurt, I hurt. Actually, I saw this coming, I just didn't know when Chester was going to pull the trigger, and I had been caught off guard. He hadn't given me a heads up, and I was grateful for that because this had to be his choice. This was his dream and his band. As his wife, it was my job to be supportive and loving.

Chester decided to work on some electronic music with a friend, a guy named Coney, who was also a friend of the Grey Daze drummer, Sean. I was so happy Chester had found a friend whom he trusted, who was supportive, and who wanted to create amazing music and some new beats. The collaboration with Coney also allowed Chester to experiment with different genres of music. He was an artist who, if given the right people and the opportunity to create, boy, he would never let anyone down. I always heard something magical in Chester's creative sessions.

I was thrilled he was already lining up other music outlets, since I was concerned that if he wasn't working on music he would be filled with sadness. Music made Chester happy. It filled his soul and was his life's purpose. What a beautiful awakening, to be so young, aware, and already know his purpose in life. He was blessed in many ways, but knowing his purpose was a huge blessing.

Purpose aside, Chester didn't get enough creative hours in with Coney due to work, and conflicts with each others schedule. He grew frustrated and said, "That's it. I'm giving up music and am going to focus on a career in real estate so I can take care of you and we can have a family."

Wow, now that was a statement! How honorable it was that my husband wanted to put his family first. I knew it wasn't going to happen, though. Music, his craft, needed to be unleashed for the sake of both his happiness and mine. You know the saying, "happy wife, happy life?" Well, that goes both ways, and I say, "Happy hubby, everyone is happy!"

It came down to a huge argument—an argument that would go down in the books and history forever. When Chester said he was giving up music to have a day job working nine to five, well, that simply wasn't going to work. Yes, he needed a job. But he also needed to continue his creative outlet. That meant he needed to continue to write music and lyrics, practice guitar, and keep his vocals warm so as not get into a rut or rusty.

Chester performed all the time and practiced several times a week when he was with his former band. "Then you owe me an hour of practice every day," I said. Yes, this was the fight. He wanted to be a family man, but deep down (or even on the surface) I knew that would never be enough for him. "You can sing to the radio, write and create music, or jam with anyone you want. But know this," I said, "you owe me an hour of practice every day or you can fight with me every day. Take your pick." I also said, "We are going to receive a phone call one year from now, and you have to be ready."

So, with my husband being held accountable by me, he practiced every day, and I could see the happiness in him. He appreciated that I pushed him and was willing to support him. And I knew if he wasn't making music and fulfilling his passion he would have been miserable, and one day would have grown resentful, even towards me.

I'm sure you're wondering why I said, "You need to be ready. You're going to get a phone call in one year." I have always listened to my intuition, and I get these flashes, or visions. This has happened to me my entire life. I do not claim to be psychic, I'm just completely in tune with my own vibrations and I always listen to my intuition. I mean always! I have learned the hard way once or twice that when I don't listen, something bad happens. I'm a quick learner, but my life is not a baseball game and there is no "three strikes, you're out" rule. No way. Receive the lesson, learn from it, and do not repeat the negative. Those are three simple steps and I do not mind following them at all.

Early in our marriage, we went on some amazing annual vacations with several of our friends in Arizona, and sometimes Celine joined us from California, along with Chester's sister, Tobi. One year, a large group of twenty to thirty of us adventured to Mexico and rented two or three private houses next to each other, right on the sand. These homes were perfect for us, and we loved waking up right on the water. It was far better then staying in a busy hotel.

These trips became a tradition, and we had the most amazing time. Life was simple, but we indulged in bonfires, the guys grilled lobsters or took us out, we romped our trucks and dirt bikes on the sand, danced the night away, and partied our asses off! That was actually an understatement, and I mean that in the most fun of ways.

We lived a very colorful life then, and were so blessed that on these trips with our best friends, family, band mates, and bosses, that when we had a diverse group come together it would be off the charts. We had the time of our lives and the wackiest trips ever. Everyone who was there could tell you their own version. Side note: To our crew, and you know who you are, I'm grateful you are all still in our lives. It may not be daily, because we all have gone on separate paths, but it's awesome that we keep in touch, and it's as if we never missed a beat.

I wanted to say that because when we got home from our insane and epic Mexico trip, the weekend we arrived back, I planned

Chester's birthday party. We were going to have fifty to seventy-five of our closest friends at our home. But, unbeknownst to us, this was the last big party we would throw at our home. As I predicted, literally to the day, we received a phone call from a man named Scott Harrington, a music industry attorney, that changed our lives forever.

Scott sent some music to us via FedEx, and we sat in the living room listening to music from a band called Xero. They were looking for a new vocalist to carry them to the next level. As we listened, Chester and I were looking at each other. our eyes getting wider. "This is the one!" I finally said.

Chester and I got on a call with Scott and Jeff Blue, who then worked at Zomba Music, and also for the band. As we discussed details, Jeff mentioned that he would like to hear Chester's voice recorded to Xero's music. He also warned us that others tried to add their own take on the already put-together band and music, and the band never liked the change in sound.

As soon as Chester and I hung up the phone, I contacted Jerry at The Phoenix Conservatory of Music to get Chester booked into the studio to record a demo. It's all about timing right? It had to be right then! We had a few problems to overcome, such as how the hell were we going to pay for it. Thank God that everyone loved Chester so much and believed in him. I called and begged, explained the situation, and gratefully they didn't make me beg too much, as the people at the studio were our friends. Everyone really pulled it together for him. The Conservatory recorded all the songs we needed for just two hundred dollars. I've said thank you, but let me put it in print and say it again. Thank you! I love you guys. It was all I had in my bank account, me being the bread winner at the time. We chose for Chester not to work much so he could remain flexible for shows or anything career-wise that came up. So, money was always tight.

After I booked Chester into the studio, I called Mark, who was one of our best friends, and said, "I need to you to take Chester to the studio, make sure the songs get recorded, then both of you get straight back to the house for his birthday party." Mark always had our backs and I could rely on him. I had a ton of people waiting to celebrate his big, twenty-third birthday bash, but business was first and I still had to handle the home front. I wanted only Mark going with Chester, and I insisted on him having no distractions. The studio was for professionals, and it wouldn't be party time until they both arrived back.

When Mark and Chester finally made it home, there were lots of big kisses, hugs, and hellos, then I started in on all the questions. I was so excited to hear about the studio. Chester explained he recorded the songs his way, the way he heard them in his head so he could sing them his way, and with passion. We got him a drink and anyone who was there and not too fucked up to actually know what was going on, heard for a first time ever, a listening party in our living room. This was of Chester, with songs from his potential new band, Xero. I was so proud of him, and I knew he was proud of the recording.

We were now going to play the music for Jeff Blue over the phone the next day, and if he or Xero didn't like Chester's voice and version, then fuck them, because Chester was proud of what he was about to share. As long as you are proud of your work and creativity, that's all that matters. Art is in the eye of the beholder and you cannot please everyone. It's important to remember that in everything we do.

Chester blew us all away that night. He was my husband, and I heard him sing all the time around the house. He always blew me away, but this time he had no prep time ahead of the recording session. He didn't write the songs, and in fact, didn't even really know them. All that would be a challenge for anyone. But, his incredible voice, determination, and passion were amazing. Chester just had the skills—skills that allow 1 percent of artists to actually make it.

I will never forget the time we went to Lake Pleasant in Arizona with several of our closest friends. Chester loved singing, all the time. For him, singing was like breathing. It was always so effortless. Plus, music made him grounded and you could actually see peace light him up on the inside. Anyway, after we all got settled and had a huge bonfire going, Chester surprised us when he broke out his acoustic guitar and began to sing "Jane Says" by Jane's Addiction.

We were all enamored by the sound of his voice and the glow from the fire lighting up his face, catching glimpses of his movement as he sang. His was the only image we saw on the dark lake. Imagine it. We are sitting along the waterfront on a lake in the middle of nowhere. Since I was from Los Angeles, I was not used to seeing so many stars. I was in such awe, trying to make out the constellations. It was pitch black, so black I could not see my hand in front of my face. Our fire was the only illumination I saw. I couldn't even see the person sitting next to me.

As we listened to the echo of Chester's voice bounce off the mountains, rocks, and water, it was as if we were each in our own universe of a perfect earthly stage, I thought we were the only people there. But, when Chester sang at the top of his lungs, belting out these songs, all popular tunes, we sat in silence as people along the shoreline around the entire lake started to applaud, whistle, and holler with excitement. They even lit up their lighters. The lake was filled with campers who just got serenaded by the soon-to-be next big thing, and all the lighters looked like twinkle lights.

We didn't know at this point if the band Xero would like Chester or his vocals, if they would accept Chester into the band, or if they would even make it. None of us had a crystal ball, but I believed in my husband and my intuition told me they would do very well.

The next morning Scott Harrington and Jeff Blue called Chester and me at our home. Jeff wanted to hear the music over the phone right then and there. We knew that wasn't going to sound nearly as good as from a quality tape, but we pushed the phone into the speaker so they could hear as clearly as possible. Fortunately, Jeff loved what he heard, and so did Scott. Jeff wanted us to FedEx the music to him that Monday but I said, "I have a better idea. How about Chester flies in with the music, and you and the band can meet him?" Of course he liked that idea, and off I went trying to pull together enough money for a Southwest airline ticket to LA for Chester. I wanted to go with him, of course, but this was an additional expense we did not have budgeted. Besides, Chester needed to meet them first. This was his big chance, I just knew it. They must have known it, too, for Chester got the gig, on a provisional basis.

The guys from Xero had a few personnel transitions going on. They were searching for just the right vocalist, and their original bass player was on tour with his first band. I believe it was a Christian rock band. Xero had a temporary musician at the time, a guy named Kyle Christner. Chester and I ended up liking Kyle and his wife, Kristen, because they were down to earth, in love, and were a little wilder than even we were. They also brought a bit of balance to the awkward dynamic between all the new people we had met. There were so many different personalities to learn how to interact with!

Chester was very different from this band in every way. For example, he hadn't grown up with everyone, so that immediate bond wasn't there. It would also take several long, agonizing months before the band was 100 percent sure if Chester was the perfect fit for them—or not.

At this time, Chester and I had been married a little over four years. What made the start with Xero hardest was the fact that we had laid roots in his hometown in Arizona, and not in California. I had the investment property that was rented, and our home that we had to sell. I was actually going to sell both, because I was so sure this would work out. Then I'd invest the proceeds into his career and to live off of until we could get situated and make our dreams and careers come true. I knew we would need all the money we could get to relocate back to Los Angeles. La La Land is an expensive place to live, so I invested the home I owned on my own, our home we bought when we were married, and every penny I had in my savings into his career.

We were also the only ones in the band who were married—at least until Scott and Penny came along. Scott Koziol replaced Kyle, until the original bassist came back. Scott was a very talented musician and Chester, Scott, Penny and I became very close friends. We related much better to them than the other band members because we were all closer in age. Plus, as the only married couples, we understood what that meant, and our responsibilities were different than those of musicians who were younger and single.

Chester and I scraped up everything we had, and risked it all by selling our two homes. If it didn't work out with Xero, we'd be sunk. I also gave up an entire career in real estate. That was fine, because we were still young enough to risk everything, and we had many discussions with regard to the decision. It was a decision we made together.

The plan was that Chester would move to LA first. We would drive back and forth several times every week, or as often as we could, to see each other while we put the houses on the market. This was quite expensive, and hard on us as a couple and on our marriage. We were used to being together all the time; it was weird. I was stuck handling the sale of the houses and putting in my notice at work, packing, and wrapping up our Arizona life. But I didn't want to stay in Arizona while Chester was in Los Angeles, in my home town without me, and all he had was a very select few of my family members to help him, along with a couple of friends. This concerned me because we had to be careful who Chester associated with while making magic happen, because we both had to make sure that the people around him actually had his best interests at heart.

Eventually, we grew tired of all the traveling and being apart, but on those long desert roads we sang, talked, and manifested. We used to pull over to the side of the road to write music and collaborate on ideas while Chester played "cowboy licks" on his guitar. Ha ha! I called them, "cowboy licks" because he could play just enough, but he was getting better everyday. However, Chester always was a master at songwriting and singing, not at playing guitar.

After a time of Chester staying at my adopted mom's condo, a friend of ours, Erin, and my cousin Celine and her husband Ernie, helped us the most. Even with a baby, Michaella, and all the chaos of the pressure of life, dreams, and careers, Celine and Ernie helped us every way they could. We were so grateful to everyone in our village who contributed to our success, and who loved and believed in us at the hardest of times. Thank you with all of my heart. We needed a little help then, and not just from our friends. They say, it takes a village, and I truly believe that.

Finally! It looked like Chester had made it into the band!

The Greatest Gift

AFTER THE BAND AGREED to accept Chester as their vocalist, we struggled and hustled to relocate, and find a way and a place to lay our heads. My dad had a room in his pool house, but my stepmonster had waited her entire life to have her first home (not a townhome) and did not want us there. Shocker! Chester and I needed to be together as husband and wife. We needed a place to call home. To be ripped apart was a huge strain—even though we knew it was part of our sacrifice.

We ended up renting a little place in Brentwood, and I got a job in real estate in the Pacific Palisades working for a title company. We were struggling more than ever, because Chester only had a coffee house job so he could remain flexible for band practice, showcases, meetings, and hopefully, a record deal and recording an album in the near future. The record deal Chester hoped to sign with Grey Daze when I first met him had never happened.

After many rehearsals, and showcase after showcase, finally something happened. Warner Bros. in LA wanted to hire Jeff Blue as their A&R (artists and repertoire) guy. Jeff agreed to take the job, as long as Warner Bros. signed Xero, the band he was working with. That was the ultimatum he made. That was huge, because Jeff put his career on the line because he so deeply believed in Chester and the band.

Holy shit, they were finally getting signed! That was one of those life changing moments for every one of us. Literally, life changing. Chester and the band had worked extremely hard on their craft. They just needed that "one" person to come along, to believe in them just as much as they believed in themselves. But that person needed to have the ability to do something about it. That was the key. Many people can believe or love what you're creating, but we all need that one person who can do something about it. Thank you Jeff, with all my heart.

♥

My cousin Celine and her husband Ernie came to our new place for a visit, and while they were there, Chester and Ernie decided to go to Santa Monica for a day. During the trip, Chester shared news of the band with Ernie, and filled him in on the current status and some obstacles they had to maneuver around. Ernie knew the band now called themselves Hybrid Theory, but what he didn't know was they would have to change their name because another band, one in the UK, already owned that name.

As they drove home Ernie looked over at a park named Lincoln Park, after President Abraham Lincoln. Ernie thought that was a great name for a band, and apparently Chester did as well. When the band got together they all shared their suggestions and he shared Lincoln Park. Trying to come up with a good band name is difficult, and in my opinion, they were all truly genius about this choice because there happened to be a Lincoln Park in nearly every metropolitan city. The band was hopeful that every fan would connect to this name, and think the band was named after the park in "their" hometown. There was only one problem. They did not own the name to President Lincoln, so they created a change in spelling and were on their way. As they became Linkin Park, they kept the name of the album they were working on as *Hybrid Theory*.

Because we were still very broke, we chose to have roommates so we could have a bigger place than our first place in Brentwood, and also have our dogs. We had to bring our family back together, which included our two canine fur babies: Sidney (after Sid Vicious, former bassist for the band the Sex Pistols) and Tashi. Bandit had gone on to doggie heaven, but Chester and I had found Sidney at the pound. When we were looking at her, Chester sat on the floor Indian-style with his legs crossed, and Sidney started to lick and nibble his ears. In that moment, Sidney became Chester's dog.

We also decided it was time for me to quit my real estate career, as I was extremely bored, and the nine to five job wasn't working for our lifestyle. I still had to work, but we both wanted my job to be flexible so that I could join Chester on tour when the time came that we could be together.

After some deliberation, I came up with an awesome idea, lol. Most people would never do this if they didn't have to, but I had never done it before, and it seemed like a lot of fun. I decided to work as a cocktail waitress at Gladstones, which was on the beach off Pacific Coast Highway and Sunset Boulevard. This was, after all, my hometown and where I grew up. I often went there as a kid with my parents, and it was our meeting place for family and friends when we had fires or mudslides, which happened more often than anyone hoped for.

So, Gladstones was a safe place for me, and we all liked to eat and drink there. Let's face it, being right on the water, nice clientele, and great food—I was sure the tips and flexible hours would be a perfect combo to pay the bills and keep me on tour with my hubby.

Thanks to Fabian, the general manager, for giving an unknown local a chance. He employed me and gave me a killer schedule. I had the freedom that Chester wanted, and still maintained my own independence. That was important to me, and I actually had a lot of fun the first month and a half. I always had an adventurous side, where I liked to experience everything. Well, almost everything, and at least once. Some call it childlike, but I call it experience.

Everything was great. I didn't trust myself to be a food server, but as a cocktail waitress, I definitely could work that! I got to meet new people, enjoy my part time job, and work only three or four days a week. Still, I was able to bring home double the money I made in my previous job in real estate. One day at work I brought a table their drinks, and all of a sudden the drinks became very heavy and I realized I was tired all the time. I thought it was from all the hustling, touring, and our late night hours.

The band started to tour and got ready to make their first video. The location was super cool, as well as a little creepy, underneath the streets of Los Angeles in an old underground railroad station that I never even knew was there. I wondered how many secrets the City of Los Angeles held? The video was coming along, but when I saw them hang Chester upside down by his feet, with tons of rocks and debris underneath him, I became really scared.

I started to cry. I was incredibly scared for Chester, but I didn't realize why I was so emotional. Thank God for Jeff's wife Carmen; she kept me calm and was a great friend in babysitting me. I say babysitting because I acted like a total baby. I was crying and scared. What the hell was wrong with me? By the way, this was the video for "One Step Closer."

A day or so later my mother-in-law, Susan, solved the mystery when she said, "Honey, I think you're pregnant." The thought had never crossed mind. All I was thinking about was how tired I was, and how everything had become so hard for me. So, I decided to

go see my doctor, Dr. Toni Long in Santa Monica, to get a pregnancy test. To my surprise, I *was* pregnant. Holy crap, Mom was
right! Oh my God, I had to tell Chester! I was scared and excited all
at the same time, with a little splash of shock thrown in.

Chester was touring, so I had to tell him the news over the
phone, which was not ideal, but I didn't have much choice. When
he found out, he was so excited that he shared the news with his
bandmates, right then and there. "I'm going to be a dad, you guys,"
he screamed. "I'm going to be a father!" When our families found
out I was pregnant, everyone was very happy with the news.

Chester was soon home off the road for a short bit, and off
to the doctor we went for an ultrasound. It was amazing to hear our
baby's heartbeat. I instantly fell in love with our child and with the
thought of becoming a mother. I thought how lucky I was to have
married my soul mate, and that we were creating a family together.
I loved Chester more right then and there, and I hadn't even known
that was possible.

Chester and I really thought we were on our way to parent-
hood, until things went terribly wrong. Dr. Long had expressed concern that the baby had not dropped all the way into my uterus. I
didn't understand. We heard the baby's heart beat. My baby was alive.
I heard him, or her. We all did! Our baby was alive and growing inside me. What did Dr. Long mean? I was both terrified and protective. I am a natural momma bear, and that protective side runs
through my veins.

Chester was back on the road performing free tours in Europe,
trying to build the band's name, brand, and music. At my follow up
appointment, the ultrasound showed the fetus (our baby) had not
dropped into my uterus and was stuck growing in my fallopian tube.
That is when Dr. Long informed me I was not having a normal
pregnancy, but an ectopic pregnancy. She said as the fetus grows he
or she will eventually burst my fallopian tube.

My only real choice was to try a new chemotherapy to make it easier for the fetus to abort naturally and pass through my fallopian tube in hopes of saving the tube for future pregnancies. That was also the most humane approach with regard to our baby. If our baby grew too much larger in my fallopian tube, he or she would suffer pain, and we would both eventually die.

Dr. Long said she had only heard of three cases with the chemotherapy, but all three were successful. I didn't have a choice. No matter what we did, our baby was not going to make it. Now we were faced with terminating our pregnancy in hopes of saving my life.

I spent a lot of time at The Self-Realization Fellowship Lake Shrine in Pacific Palisades. This was my church and I prayed and meditated for hours on end. I needed peace and quiet. I knew our baby chose Chester and me as his or her soul group, but was not ready to be earthly bound. I believe that babies (souls) choose their parents. This soul chose us. However, I believe this soul didn't choose earth. I know in my heart that my baby is one of my guardian angels. Thank you Angel Baby. Our souls are connected and I know we will be together in all our collective energy, always. With light and love, your earthly mommy.

It's so hard for me to share this, since it was such a scary time. Chester was on tour, but I was lucky that our roommate, Jay, went with me to my chemo appointment. I was terrified, but he held my hand while the doctor gave me the injection of chemotherapy. It didn't hurt much physically; the pain I felt was a shattered heart. To be clear, it was one injection and it immediately terminated our baby, pain free. That was one of the saddest days of my life. I was pregnant for more than three months and my hormones were all over the place. I was so emotional and was in uncharted territory.

Thank goodness Chester's mom came to be with me. According to Susan, I was doing well at first, but then I began to spot (bleed). Then the bleeding stopped and we thought all was good. That is when Mom thought I was in the clear and decided to head back to Arizona.

My younger brother Alex was about to turn thirteen and have his Bar Mitzvah, the Jewish ceremony for a boy coming of age and going into manhood. It was a very special day for my brother, as he had been attending Hebrew School, and according to Jewish law, when a Jewish boy becomes thirteen years old he then becomes accountable for his actions.

I didn't have a Bat Mitzvah, which is the ceremony for girls. I'm not Jewish by birth and didn't show any interest in the religion, although I find it very beautiful. I like to take bits and pieces from all religions, but do not believe in just one. There is beauty in all things, including all religions, and we should take what resonates with us individually and apply it to our lives—if that makes us happy and if it helps us become better people.

Unlike a wedding, where people sometimes get divorced and remarried, a Bar Mitzvah only happens once in a boy's lifetime. There was no way I wasn't going to be there for my baby brother. I loved him and was so proud of him. Family is the most important thing to me, even if I sometimes had to deal with my stepmonster. Even as the black sheep, I had bonded with my younger brothers, no matter our age differences.

At my next doctor appointment, Dr. Long said things looked good and the miscarriage would probably begin soon. I was to take it as easy as possible, but this was said before I told her about my younger brother's bar mitzvah and how I had to be there. I'm pretty sure there was some begging involved, because it was against her better judgment to let me go.

I am so glad I went, though. The event was amazing, and my dad even got me a room at the Crowne Plaza Redondo Beach and Marina where the bar mitzvah reception was being held in the evening, after the ceremony at the temple earlier that morning. That was so generous and kind of him. I really appreciated it, because I didn't know how I might feel. If I needed to lie down, now I had a place to go. I also wasn't sure if I would be able to make it home or not, so the hotel room was a perfect back up plan.

Everyone on my dad's side of the family came out to celebrate my brother turning into a man. There were tons of cousins, and I decided to drink my pain and sadness away. Besides, I wanted to have the best time I could with my family. I sat out a lot of dances but did get out on the floor for one mellow song. If I participated even a little, no one would have a pity party for me, I thought. This was my brother's day, and I didn't want to take away from his moment.

Sadly, I overheard a family member in the woman's bathroom say I was either faking it, or trying to get attention. As if? I can't believe anyone could say or think such disturbing things. Of course, the words came out of my lovely stepmonster's mouth, and were said to her equally lovely sister. They were two peas in a pod. Meanwhile, my husband and I had to terminate our child. Hello assholes, we just had to kill our baby you fucking twats! Okay, God, that felt good to say. Moving along, I still wasn't in the clear medically myself. I was here against my doctor's wishes. To my brothers, if haven't told you enough, Alex and David, there's nothing in this world I wouldn't do for either of you. That includes you, too, Scotty.

As the night progressed, thank God for my cousin Carrie and her then boyfriend. Both knew I wasn't feeling well; they could see it on my face. Carrie said she took one look at me and knew she needed to get me up to my hotel room, fast. They both sat with me to see if I was going to be okay, and as I rested I said, "I just want to be back in my own bed, in our Brentwood apartment."

So, they drove me home, helped me up the flight of stairs, got me situated with water and pain pills, and tucked me into bed.

My father-in-law, Lee, whom I called Pops, came to stay with me while Chester was in Europe. I still had some cramping, but my doctor said that was normal, so we were not concerned. I called Susan, "Mom," a few days later in tears. My cramps were so bad and the pain was alarmingly fierce. I actually don't remember making the call, but Susan does. Susan knew all that was going on medically because she was my mother-in-law, and she also worked in the medical field.

Apparently, I told her that Lee refused to take me to the hospital, and that's when Susan demanded to talk to him, to explain the urgency. Lee said I wasn't taking enough pain medication. He was right. I couldn't take what my doctor prescribed, even though the pain was severe. It was a heavy dose every three to four hours and made me remember things differently. I also had passed out after taking it, not knowing for how long. I didn't even know what day it was.

Susan told him he should take me to the hospital *now*. I think he really wanted me to do as the doctor prescribed before rushing me to the hospital, though. There was one moment that was clear for me, however. Lee was standing at the foot of my bed, looking at me with fear in his eyes. That was the moment he realized I was dying. I was so out of it that I wasn't afraid, at least not until I looked up into his eyes. Chester's father had fear in his eyes, and I saw it. That was a clear indicator, and I knew right then that I would not live without immediate medical attention.

My adopted parents were nowhere around, even though they lived in Redondo Beach. Instead, Chester's parents from Arizona were taking care of me—all three of them! Thank God for Susan, Lee, and Susan's husband, Alan. Susan finally told Lee that if I died, it was on him. He must have snapped to as I began to convulse in my bed. Next thing I knew he had scooped me up and was rushing me to the Providence Saint John's Health Center in Santa Monica.

Right away, the doctors there took me into emergency surgery. It turned out that I was bleeding internally, badly, and the fetus was half in my fallopian tube and half in my abdomen. That meant that I was drowning in my own blood. Were we having fun yet? That also explained the pain I felt as blood started to fill into my lungs. I had less then twenty-four hours to live.

The doctors removed my entire right fallopian tube, because it was badly damaged. I do remember that Lee's was the last face I saw before surgery and the first face I saw when I woke up. Thank you Pops, Susan, Dr. Toni Long, and Dr. Marie Ottavi. I'm extremely grateful to you and your staff for saving my life.

When I woke up to find Lee was there, it was very comforting. Then my dad showed up, which was a surprise. I had wanted my dad there earlier, but guessed that he was busy and came when he could. Luckily, I made it through surgery. Twenty minutes after visiting with my dad, very much to my surprise, Chester walked in. I was confused, because he was in Europe on tour. How could he arrive twenty minutes after my dad?

Turned out that Susan and Lee had filled Chester in on the details, and he took the next flight out. Sixteen hours later, here he was. After awakening from surgery it was so wonderful to have my husband by my side. It meant the world to me, but I also knew he had to go back and join his band mates. I would slowly recover, but everyone in the band had worked so hard and there were five other business partners who needed their lead vocalist to help them continue to build their careers.

There was not much Chester could do for me that anyone else couldn't do. Now it was just a matter of time before I healed and recovered. I also didn't like him seeing me like that. Selfishly, I wanted him to stay, but I pushed him to go back on the road. That was just one of the many times that Chester put our family and me first. He made me feel so much love and I appreciated all that he sacrificed for me during those dark days. I know he was torn between his wife and his career, but he handled both with class, even with strong business pressures. I appreciated him for showing up, and for loving me in that moment of time when I needed it, and him, the most.

I spent a few days in the ICU and received several units of blood (maybe four or five). It was going to take time before I could gather strength enough to walk, and that's when Susan and I figured out that I could not take care of our dogs. I could barely take care of myself. Susan stepped in and took care of me after the hospital, and when she went home, Alan came to bring the dogs home to Flagstaff, where they stayed for several months while I recuperated.

Here comes the "fun" part. All my hormones were out of whack. I was pregnant through the first trimester, and now I wasn't. I was extremely emotional, and heartbroken over the loss of our child. I wasn't the only one, either. Chester was ready and determined to be a father. This made me so happy. Between Chester's tours we started our research and began the process, with the help of our regular doctor, of finding a fertility specialist.

Dr. Long initially suggested we seek out a fertility specialist due to the fact that one of my fallopian tubes had been removed, and the other was small, with tissue grown together fusing it completely closed. There was absolutely no way anything could pass through my one remaining tube. After several painful procedures that tried to flush my tube to clear it for the possibility of a natural pregnancy, not even a single drop of liquid could pass through. It was clear that I would never again become pregnant with out the help of a specialist. Through all this, I also learned that all of my organs are very tiny. Who knew?

Dr. Hal Danzer was the fertility specialist referred to us, and I quickly fell in love with him. His bedside manners and staff (especially Dusta) were fabulous. He drew my blood every week at least once, and sometimes several times, to be sure all levels were healthy for my baby and for me. Dr. Danzer is known worldwide for his results in creating beautiful, successful, healthy families, and people from around the world come to see him as their fertility specialist.

After our first meeting with Dr. Danzer, Chester and I decided he was the doctor for us. I was in the greatest hands in his Beverly Hills office twice a week. I was there so often, they saw me more than my family and friends did. I'm not going to lie. It was a very difficult process. Two shots a day in my stomach, and one a day in my hip, alternating hips every other day. I was covered in bruises, which wasn't a very hot look, but was well worth it for our future baby!

What was so incredible, was that Dr. Danzer knew the exact two-week period that I should take a daily baby aspirin, which stopped the Lupus gene from being passed to our baby. Lupus ran in both our families. That was such a huge health benefit, and of course was important to both Chester and me. We could also choose when the baby would be born, by choosing the time of conception, so were able to plan for our baby to be born when Chester was off tour.

The fertility process continued while Chester went back on the road. Early on, Chester and I decided I should be with him as much as possible so he could experience much of our pregnancy, but flying with medicines and daily shots that were temperature sensitive was stressful for me. Actually, not just for me, but for everyone around us. Everyone helped, though. We even needed doctor's notes and dry ice. Everything had to be at the perfect temperature always, and the shots had to be administered at the exact same time everyday. It was a bit of a shit show in airports, trying to explain why I had syringes—and in different sizes.

At one point, I flew to hang with my besties in New York. My friend Stacey and I initially met on tour at Jones Beach in New York.

Her brother is Perry Ferrel from the band Jane's Addiction. Stacey and I became friends, and that was a wrap. Insta besties.

Now, Stacey and I met up with another special friend, Luke. Luke and I had met through a pop band and became so close that when he was in LA we spent time hanging, and when I was in NY we always visited. He was my emotional support before and during my pregnancy, and when I struggled with my marriage. Joining, Stacey, Luke, and me was Chester's sister, Tobi.

I wanted to take these few days to spend with my friends, and then I was off to meet Chester on tour. I was so grateful for my friends and family, because I was terrified of needles and couldn't give myself the shots at first. My cousin David helped me in California when I was at home. He is a doctor, so he taught me and helped administer my shots. When I was in New York, Stacey and Luke helped me until I joined Chester, and he took over from there. I took *in vitro* very seriously. I wanted to be one of the best patients ever, so I listened and did exactly what the doctor told me. Well, almost exactly. I get like that when I trust someone and my intuition doesn't tell me to run! Here, I fully trusted all my doctors.

I was still taking shots in the middle of a Linkin Park World Tour, the first Project Revolution Tour in 2002, when Chester's bus generator broke down. That meant no refrigerator, and my medicine needed to be at the perfect temp! Chester and I panicked, as did the band's tour manager. Thank God for the many friends who were touring with us, because it was Jonathan Davis, the lead singer of Korn, who let me fill up the refrigerators on their private buses with all my medications that needed to be kept at different temperatures. I will be forever grateful.

The band toured a lot, but I was with Chester more than I wasn't. Everyone we toured with became family. Yes, some closer than others, and some we toured with multiple times. We all lived and worked together, traveling from city to city, state to state, and even country to country. When that happens, the people you spend time with really do become family.

Our new family of friends were there for us in both our day-to-day and our business lives. Together, we all became a fusion of love. When a person needed support in an AA meeting, someone was there. We all also shared and reveled in birthday and anniversary celebrations.

Chester and I even ran into other families on the road who were trying to get pregnant. Members of other bands sometimes saved our ass in so many ways. One even rescued me off a private jet when I was walking down a runway by myself, towing all my luggage, and wearing my hubby's boxers and a wife beater T-shirt. I was completely out of my mind and wasn't even clear where I was because the night before we were dancing to "Missy Elliot, Get Your Freak On" while flying in the air and having cocktails. On this plane ride I decided for the first time to take something to sleep and I woke up really fuzzy and confused. As my friends thought it was pretty funny, I assume, they kept me safe!

By the way, a huge shout out to the band Papa Roach for saving me the morning after we landed. I was exhausted and had no clue where we were. Thank you for the ride to the hotel and getting me there safely. I love each and every one of you, especially my girl Kelly, founder and lead singer Jacoby Shaddix's wife.

For me, the greatest thing about touring was connecting with people who had many of the same interests. I felt that with every individual I met, no matter what their title is, was, or was about to be—president of the record label, bus driver, tour manager, vocalist, bassist, drummer, production, bodyguard, sound, lighting, PA (personal assistant). It didn't matter. It definitely took a village to keep each person going, to keep each person on track, and focused on his or her strengths. It was truly an honor to work with and get to know everyone.

Finally, we came home. Now it was time to see if the fertility drugs had worked, and if I was pregnant. OMG. Drum roll, please! Off to Dr. Danzer's I went to take yet another blood test with Dusta, but this time I was so excited because it was a pregnancy blood test. Dusta could have done anything to me that day and I would not have cared. This was the tell all test, but I didn't learn the results right away. The doctor was going to call later to let me know if I was pregnant or not. I was on pins and needles and so bummed that I couldn't find out the news immediately, but I had to wait so I gathered my stuff and headed home.

I was not more than five minutes down the road when Dusta called me on my cell. I was so happy to hear from him right away, and scared at the same time. Why was *he* calling, and not the doctor? Was something wrong? It is a wonder how many crazy thoughts can run through your mind in seconds. I could hardly believe it when Dusta shouted, "Congratulations. You're pregnant! You have to pretend to hear the news first hand when Dr. Danzer calls you."

"Thank you, thank you, thank you!" I screamed, crying at the same time. These were the happiest of tears.

The first call I made was to Chester, who was on the road again. Chester screamed from the rooftops that he was going to be a father, and we both cried and felt completely blessed. The *in vitro* worked on our first try! I so love Dr. Danzer, Dusta, and the nurses who helped us. I told them that all the time, even when I was under a twilight sedation. I took being pregnant extremely seriously, just as I did *in vitro*. Now, here I was, grateful beyond my wildest dreams.

After I learned the wonderful news, I stopped dying my hair and getting acrylic nails. I did not want to use any product that wasn't completely natural. Due to *in vitro* and the doctors monitoring everything my body needed, I didn't have any crazy cravings. The one thing I did want was milk and I didn't normally drink milk, so I just followed what my body wanted. I also had my baby's name planned from a very young age. The good news was, we'd get to put the name to good use. Dr. Long eventually told us we were pregnant with a boy, Draven Sebastian Bennington. God bless that our prayers were answered.

Love Note

Dear Dad,

I'm writing to you because I do not know what else to do, or how to express my feelings. When mom got sick so long ago is when things went downhill for us. We were very close Dad; we were buddies. Every Sunday we had father and daughter racquetball days and I always looked forward to our time together. You were all I had, Dad, and I felt safe with you then. You adopted me and I'm still your only daughter. We even had our father/daughter song by Oscar Brown, Jr.: Hey daddy what dat dare / And why that over dare / and oh hey daddy can I have that pink elephant over dare. I sing that song regularly, and Oscar Brown, Jr. will always be my favorite jazz artist. Thanks for teaching me jazz and the blues.

Over the years you created a new life for yourself and didn't stick up for me at all. You betrayed me and abandoned me. Throughout my childhood I got used to you hurting me and letting me down. Now, as an adult, and as I have become a parent myself, I do not understand how you could treat your child the way you have treated me. Actually, it makes me sick to my stomach. I could never turn my back on my son, especially if he was hurting or in need of my help.

Let's be honest, Dad. I never did anything so wrong to deserve the treatment you and your wife have given me throughout my life. I could care less how you justify buying and adopting a child, only to end it with abandonment and cruelty. I was a normal teen. Normal. You can paint the picture however you want, but I will shine through all the ugliness.

During the summer, you always shipped me off to camp so I would not have to be with you or your wife. I can finally thank you for that now, although personally, I would never do that to my child. I chose to be a mother and was blessed through *in vitro* to have my son—just as you chose to be a parent when you were blessed with adopting a child when you and my adopted mom could not have any children. I choose to look at the silver lining of this situation, and for me, it was becoming super independent at the age of twelve. I also became an amazing mother.

You did teach me the basics of business, and how to manage a checkbook at a very young age. You also helped me a little here and there when I was struggling on my own. Thanks, but my friends became my family and helped me more than you did, and they still do. I know who my family and friends are, and who has Draven and my best interests at heart. The abandonment gave me a fight and flight mode that serves me well and protects me. By default, I thank you for that.

Now you want to be a part of our lives, and every time I let you back in it's the same situation. Our father/daughter relationship is dictated by how your wife sees fit. She is my nemesis. I will not allow you to come into my and my son's life whenever its convenient for you. Family isn't always convenient. It's about being there for your loved ones, and being family through the good times and bad.

You also never believed in me or Chester. You never helped my husband, even when you had the means to do so. You had plenty of room at your new home, a home with rooms with their own entrance. But, you chose to not help your only daughter and only son-in-law. We only needed a place to crash temporarily, and we didn't need you to help us financially. We needed help and you had a guest room in your pool house.

I needed my family so badly then. I was struggling, trying to pay for two houses. One was rented out, but with property taxes on both houses and only one income (mine) while having roommates and Chester focusing on the band full time, we barely survived. We had roommates so we could have a little extra money to fly back and forth to see each other while Chester was trying to make musical history. We struggled to sell the houses, to pay our bills, and we needed both of our families.

You weren't there to help, but you and your wife were both there for the success, the parties, and whenever you both felt you had bragging rights. Dad, I know you love us, but the way you love us is really fucked up.

You and I have tried to have a separate relationship with each other—and without your wife—over the years. It was a nice thought to move past the pain, and try to have a healthy relationship. That will never work out now. I have zero respect for you, as you never stood up for me as a father should, and you allowed your wife to manipulate your relationship with me, your only daughter. No one has ever hurt me as much as you did, and that's because I loved you the most. Or I did at one time.

One of the worst times was when my grandfather died. You called to tell me, and Draven, who was nine, and I got ready for the funeral. Then you called and left a message on my answering machine that we were uninvited because my presence would make my stepmonster unhappy. Really? What kind of dad un-invites his daughter to her own grandfather's funeral? I still find it hard to believe you did that.

My son and I are pretty amazing human beings, and we are far better off not seeing you again. It's definitely your loss. It's a loss for me because I still love you, and hope for acceptance, but I will never give you an opportunity to crush our hearts and you will never have a chance to come in and out of our lives again. My son barely knows you, and as long as I can protect him he has no desire to have you in his life. I'm upset at myself for allowing you to disappoint us so many times in the past as you came in and out of our lives seemingly on a whim. Every time I hope for a different outcome, just like a silly little girl who is a fool. It truly is a definition of insanity, repeating the same pattern and expecting different results.

It's my job as a mother, so it's best for all of us to say goodbye. I'm sorry this is painful, but Dad, I let you go with light and love.

I will protect my son from as much pain and suffering as possible. It's sad to say, we have to let you go. You no longer have a daughter or grandson.

I will always love you, but this is good bye.

Sam

The Three O's

OUR LIVES WERE ABOUT to change drastically with a baby on the way, careers in full effect, and non-stop touring. Our lives were changing so fast, but I cannot express how happy I was that we were having a baby, a wonderful, loved addition to our family. I knew it was going to be hard to tour while pregnant (and tour with a baby on board). And, I could not imagine the specifics, only that it would be very different. I hoped this little angel would light up our lives. We would find out soon enough, but I already knew that my baby had already lit up my soul.

It was difficult to have to continue the progesterone shots after I found out I was pregnant. I thought once I was pregnant the shots would stop, but apparently I needed the hormone. I knew the shots were going to add a little more pressure to the traveling, but hey, we've got this. I've got this!

What was so awesome was that so many of the wives who were blessed to be on the same tour together ended up pregnant at the same time. The music industry was having a bit of a baby boom, so it was a relief for me to share the experience. How exciting and scary being pregnant can be! Especially with emotions all wrapped up, and a first pregnancy. Being pregnant and away from family and friends was hard enough, but on the road, in a different state every day, and some days in a different country, it was much harder. When faced with a new environment, at first it was weird, but then it became the norm. New place, same routine. Get on a bus or a plane, wake up, and you're there—wherever there may be.

Really though, these beautiful women whom I became friends with, our friendships developed over many tours and many hours spent together. Some wives I met for the first time, only to find we had several connections. To begin with, our husbands were musicians who were famous, and there was a lot that came with that. We also had the fact that many of us were first time moms. Over the years, some of these woman have stayed in my day-to-day life, and others I see whenever life brings us together. But, I share beautiful, very special bonds with them, that of friendship, and the shared experience of life.

Thank you ladies for sharing mommy tips, fears, excitement, laughter, and so much love and joy. A huge shout out to Mary with Stone Temple Pilots, Kelly with Papa Roach, Vanessa with Stained, and Nina with No Doubt. They each made touring seem normal, and just a thing that we did. We girls had so much in common. Lots of tea and hot cocoa for starters. That was my guilty pleasure when I was pregnant, hot cocoa, and now I was allergic to milk chocolate. Some think it's awful to be allergic to chocolate, but I say my ass is grateful!

When we first found out I was pregnant, my doctor didn't want me to fly in my first trimester. That was a big problem. Was Dr. Danzer serious? How on earth could I be with my husband when his career required me to travel? The doctor then put me on bed rest, so I had to stay home. All I can say is, I don't know how to rest.

Neither of us saw the bed rest coming. I was so in the moment of getting pregnant and relishing in the fact that I was, actually, pregnant. I didn't think about touring or flying at all, even though that was a new normal for us. I thought God was playing a dirty trick on me, or reminding me that He had answered all of my prayers regarding Draven. I often think, "Do not be greedy, Sam. God and the Universe have blessed you and have always answered your wishes. Stay in gratitude." It was a good reality check that I needed to stay in my moment and appreciate one thing fully at a time. Let's face it, God/Source answered me every time I asked.

Back to business and reality. OMG! Bed rest meant I would miss our very first time at the Video Music Awards! I thought *I* was upset, but that was an understatement because Chester was more upset than I was. He was so clear that he wanted his wife by his side. I understood. It was his first VMA show, appearance, and nomination. This was in 2002 and was his first Grammy win. They won Best Hard Rock Performance. It was such a huge deal for him and I was sad that I couldn't be there to support him. I knew he needed me. I was his best friend, after all. And, I was his wife. Thank God for Tobi who stepped in to join him at the event.

The Grammy was just one result of Chester's growing popularity and fame. Linkin Park had quickly developed into one of the top bands in the world, and had millions of fans. Chester was now often recognized when we went out, and we had to sometimes think carefully about where we went, and when, so as to still have some sense of normalcy and privacy.

Want to hear one of the sweetest stories? I always had a few favorite female vocalists, all of whom possessed different types of talent and evoked different emotions in me. At the VMAs that year, not only was my husband going to perform, but so was Nikka Costa, an Australian-American singer whose music combined pop, soul, and blues. I was so bummed not to see her perform live and meet her. I had always admired her. Well, Draven came first without a doubt.

My family and friends all came to our home in Pacific Palisades Highlands, the same house we lived when the MTV show, *Cribs,* filmed a tour of it. Because I couldn't go to the VMAs, we decided to have an award show party. Thank you to everyone who came. I still appreciate the support and want to give a special shout out to Mark from Hed PE and Pamella, a.k.a. Pamilá! That was the nickname Chester gave her, he was so funny and animated that when he came up with a nickname it generally stuck—and it stuck with Pamella. But, he was the only one who could get away with teasing her in that manner.

Half way through the day of the award show and party I got a phone call from Chester. "Babe," he said. "I have someone here who would like to speak to you."

I couldn't imagine who might want to talk to me. Then a sweet, soft voice said, "Hello, honey."

"Who is this?" I asked.

"Honey, it's Nikka," the soft voice said.

"OMG, shut up!" I could hardly believe it. Then I finally gathered my wits about me. "Nikka, honey, you are so sweet to call."

Nikka told me how Chester asked if she would call to say hello. He had told her that I was a huge fan of her music, and why I wasn't there. "All he talked about was you, and how you are having a baby," she said. Then she added that she was moved by our story.

After she asked how I was feeling, she wished me congratulations. Then I told her how I adored her music, and how the phone call was incredibly kind of them both. Really, it was so thoughtful and lifted my spirits completely. Thank you, Nikka, I will never forget that beautiful memory, or the beautiful way Chester set it up.

It's hard being young and married, especially when one or both people are in the entertainment business. I think only about 1 percent of the population makes it to the top in the business, or are even semi-successful at their craft. The pressure is insane. It is rewarding, but being pushed and pulled in every direction, and satisfying the demands that come with that, no one can prepare enough for all the changes that come. To all the entertainers in the world who are married, my hat goes off to you.

Just like other married couples, Chester and I had good, bad, and some down right hard times. We signed up for all of it, but it didn't help when times were tough and the world was watching. There were many moments in our life when I not only felt married to my husband, I also felt married to the band.

In addition, there were other people we had to consider, people who saw more of our lives than fans, but were not in our day-to-day life. Just as with your job and your co-workers, they do not know everything or see everything in your life, and you do not know everything about them. We all get a glimpse of each others lives, but it's only a glimpse.

When you own your own business, any kind of business, it's like having a second marriage. That was the difference between Linkin Park and Grey Daze. Grey Daze was not a marriage. Chester grew up with the Grey Daze guys, and so did I, in my early twenties. That dynamic, along with those band mates, were different. We grew up together as kids and young adults, and had strong friendships that built a foundation that carried us through life.

I have a theory that what you like in your twenties you most often do not like in your thirties. We all grow and change, but there is always the exception. I was twenty-nine and getting ready to have my first child, and with my challenges in pregnancy, most likely my only child. Then add in distance, lots of traveling, and tons of people pulling at you, and pulling at your husband's fame. There were my hormones, money, drugs, alcohol, sex, adultery, the music industry, new band mates, and most important, the fans.

Let's not forget the fanatics who never met me, and even if they had in a brief moment, did not know me but are more opinionated about me than my own mother and father! Those are just some of the lovely ingredients no one knows about or can understand until they have experienced it. Let me know how smoothly your marriage goes when faced with the things we were faced with constantly. Read those words with a facetious tone and a behind-the-scenes giggle!

Were Chester and I perfect? Not at all. Were we like other human beings, fighting for our marriage and family? Yes. This was our time, and for the most part it was a very happy time. Bumpy? Yes. I have shared many reasons as to why. Enough said.

I'm not a political person. As I always said, "I'm a pippy," meaning I think of myself as a punk rock hippy. Not only do I not like politics, I especially do not like politics in my personal life. In business, there are more politics than I like to admit. I'm speaking for me, and as a voice for my immediate family. But when business bleeds into my personal life, that is when the punk rock girl in me surfaces. Although, I have to admit I do like the "hip-pity dip-pity" way of looking at things. Let love rule!

Baby showers, weddings, invites to housewarmings, holiday parties, and "wow," industry politics, played a huge part in our business, and bled into our personal lives. I wanted to be selfish and enjoy my pregnancy. I was in my present moment, a mama bear right out of the gate. The moment I found out I was pregnant I became so protective. I didn't like to be touched by anyone who didn't ask first. I didn't want photos taken of me or my giant baby bump. I didn't want to be fake. It's not my style, and I didn't like being forced to share special, private moments with people I was forced to be around for one reason or another. Just because Chester worked with certain people didn't mean I always got along with them, or even liked them.

That's a good life lesson we all eventually discover. We all have to grow up at some point and bite our tongues for the greater good. It's like the lesson of patience for me. Ugh. We are adulting now! Are we having fun yet?

♥

Draven was ready to be born early. He kept trying to come into the world before he was ready, and we kept him in the womb as long as we could to make sure his lungs were fully developed. But, there came a point where there was no room for him in my belly anymore. He was so tall already that when he kicked me he knocked the wind out of me. When it came to be delivery time, Draven was born four weeks earlier then our scheduled due date.

We did have a scheduled C-section, because if I had been able to go full term, Draven would have weighed nine or ten pounds. That would have required a C-section for sure. At five-foot-one, my body was too tiny for our big, healthy, baby boy. He was born premature, but naturally, I'm proud to say. In the last four weeks of pregnancy a baby grows half an inch to an inch every week. Draven was a huge, fully developed preemie, and weighed in at five and a half pounds.

I actually got into a spiritual trance on the delivery table. It's so funny that our family and friends thought I would be screaming and cussing. Instead, I was calm, making jokes, and telling the nurses not to worry. "Chester will sign autographs for you after the baby is born," I said just before I went into a meditative flow.

Chester and I had made it through only one Lamaze class, and when Draven was ready to meet the world his head was centered down my backbone. I wasn't prepared for back labor at all! Back labor is so painful. People say you forget the pain, but that's crazy. I didn't forget the pain of childbirth, but I would have done it a hundred times over again for Draven. I only allowed two people in the room with me, and yes, I was terrified. Celine held one of my legs and Chester held the other.

I will never forget when Draven was born because Dr. Long said as soon as Draven came into this world, "Well, we know who the father is!" Draven from birth was a carbon copy of his dad. It was a joke, knowing we had him through *in vitro*, but right out of the womb he was the splitting image of his father.

We started to travel with Draven when he was two months old. Thank God for my friend Stacey. She, being the closest of my best friends, came to LA to save the day, and helped us as our assistant. This all happened without any of us thinking things all the way through, and none of us took a look as to what would be best for her and for us.

It's always hard to work with your best friends. Business and friendship lines get blurred. Stacey knows this, but I hope she reads this and knows I love her with all my heart. I'm so grateful she was a part of our lives. We are blessed knowing that our friendship will last a lifetime and has made it through the best of times and some of the worst times. I love and thank Stacey for helping me navigate through some very life-changing moments.

Stacey came to live with us in a new house we bought in Redondo Beach off of Ave. C and Pacific Coast Highway. I was so over the moon with happiness and really wanted my best friend by my side. Chester and I decided before we gave birth to Draven that we should move closer to my dad and brothers, to live near some of our family.

My mom still lived in Redondo Beach, too. Chester and I helped her get into an assisted independent living place and paid her rent for nearly two years. I thought living near my mom, grandpa and two uncles was the way to go. My dad was the closest grandparent, and for our son to have two uncles close by, within five min-

utes of us, was going to be amazing. Of course with Chester's growing fame, my stepmonster became increasingly friendly. It's funny
how people change over status or money.

One problem we ran into moving from the Palisades Highlands
to Redondo Beach was the lack of privacy. Our new, three-story
front duplex with a little yard with the perfect white picket fence
that we built was only two blocks from the beach. That sounds great,
right? Well, every fan who found out where we lived decided to
come over or drive by, screaming out their car windows or sunroof
for us to come out of our home.

After having Draven, fans left gifts on our doorstep or pulled
into our driveway blasting Linkin Park music. This caused several
car accidents and we decided after less than eight months to move
to Palos Verdes, and to find a home that would facilitate our privacy
needs and still let us be close to family.

We had been house hunting for some time when we pulled into
a house that was so hidden by a private driveway that when driving
down the street people wouldn't even realize a house was there. That
was exactly what we were looking for. I prayed that the inside fit our
needs just as much.

Stacey, Chester, Draven, and I pulled up the driveway with our
business manager and realtors leading the way, and all I could see
were the garage doors and the front door. Once we were parked in
the driveway no one could see our cars from the street. Chester and
I looked at each other and knew a silent prayer had been answered.

As we took our first steps into the house, I took a quick scan
and knew right then that this was the house I had been manifesting
and dreaming about. As I walked down the long, wooden hallway
floor, and made my way to the door between the kitchen and dining
room, I looked outside and saw an avocado tree over the Jacuzzi.
That's when I looked at Chester and said, "We have to buy this
house, and if you don't want to buy it, I will buy it on my own."

Chester knew I was serious, but after the walk through, he also fell in love with the house. This was my dream home! Draven was approximately two months old and this was the house I was going to raise our son in—one way or another.

When Chester and I drove back and forth from Arizona to California in the late nineties, transitioning and moving from one state to another, I used to daydream and manifest the life I wanted to live. I imagined with extreme detail what my home looked like. I had so much fun creating my dream home and lifestyle in my mind. It was thrilling to find out that I was able to manifest this amazing house! Of course, we bought it.

When we were settled in our new home, I decided to go back to dancing, and felt a pull toward modern jazz or hip hop. So, I joined a hip hop class to help me get back into shape after having Draven. I even joined a burlesque/hip hop squad, and Chester was completely supportive. Although, I'm sure after that one fun night that he emceed for us, I don't think he really wanted his wife at rehearsals, practicing around the clock, and performing.

I loved to dance the way Chester loved to sing, so to say he didn't want me to perform was soul crushing. But I understood. Besides, dancing was my passion, not my career. It also took me awhile to bounce back and regain my confidence, flexibility, and overcome my stage fright. Yes, I still had an extreme amount of stage fright. No one would gather that, because I'm such an extravert. However, put me in the spotlight and I just want to puke.

I was determined to work off the baby fat, but was struggling because the wind was constantly getting knocked out of me every time I worked out. Many of my muscles had become detached when I gave birth. Draven was so long and strong he actually disconnected my muscles on the inside. Part of my workouts now consisted of taking Draven with me to the beach for a skate/workout while pushing him in his stroller. I was so ambitious and I've always loved the outdoors. Working out is a form of grounding myself both ener-getically and spiritually, and is my time away from phones and computers.

I met an amazing trainer named Leisha, at the beach on a day she was training a class. She has since become one of my closest friends, and her older daughters, Alexis and Megan, became Draven's first babysitters. The girls were a major help and having great babysitters was the key to me having some "me time." I tried my hardest to get back to my normal, tiny self, and was almost to my goal of trimming back down, but something was still off and I struggled with my breathing.

In 2002, when Draven was four months old, Linkin Park was about to record their second album. When my husband was record-ing an album, I left town for a few days. It kept the peace. Recording an album takes many long hours, and is sometimes extremely frus-trating for an artist. I'm not anyone's emotional punching bag, and Chester was an emotional artist. As his wife, I often bore the brunt of his verbal outbursts.

So, I gave him space to not have family pressures when he recorded. Then our fights became the "I miss you fight" instead of him taking the day-to-day studio grind out on yours truly. It wasn't that he meant to. Like many people, Chester was harder on the ones he loved because he thought they loved him so much they would put up with his shit. I'm not going to start pointing fingers. I know I'm guilty of doing the same. But, maybe because I did love him so much I made excuses for his behavior.

With a new album in the works, Stacey, Draven, and I went off to Hawaii, to the island of Maui. Chester took a long weekend break between recording and touring, and he and I privately and quietly renewed our wedding vows.

One day at the pool, before Chester arrived, I ran into Tobin Esperance, the bass player for Papa Roach. He was there with his wife, Jen. We had been on tour with Papa Roach many times and I was thrilled to find that Tobin and Jen were celebrating their honeymoon. So, I asked them to join Chester and me as we renewed our vows, and asked them to be our witnesses. Stacey would of course be there, too. It was so beautiful to share this moment with such great friends, and it all came together organically. None of us knew the others would be there. During our renewal, we released a dozen butterflies, and our baby boy was a part of our ceremony, too. The beach, my happy place, was a perfect place to get married again.

We did not expect paparazzi, or footage being released to MTV before we could tell our family, friends, and the band. But, that's what happened. Our business managers didn't even know what we were up to. Nice and private, or so we thought. Nevertheless, it was perfect, and a beautiful experience. Our new vows were our way of forgiving all the negative words and everything else we ever may have done over the years to hurt each other. We also made the choice of love by marrying each other again. In that moment I really believed that would make everything better.

Just a few months earlier, at the VMA show in New York, when Draven was only two months old, our marriage had turned very rocky. I think men are used to wives doting on them. Then, when a child is born, the baby gets almost all the attention. That was hard on us, and over the years I'd been faced with the part of stardom where if I didn't give Chester attention, someone else would have. He actually said that I was insecure for questioning his behavior—when I had good reason to. Other women tried to come into our marriage and actually called me.

Then, I think any wife would question her marriage and stand up for herself. I laugh at the notion of being insecure, because anyone who knows me knows that adjective is not in my vocabulary, or even in my DNA.

When we were in New York for the VMA awards, Chester and I went out for dinner and drinks as a date night at the W Hotel. I decided to not drink much, but kept ordering cocktails for him. My plan was to get him drunk and have the "truth serum" tell me everything. We had a lovely dinner and he was pretty buzzed when I said that I loved him very much and wasn't going anywhere. Then I asked, "How do you do it?"

"Do what?" he asked.

"I've known for some time," I said, "but you need to be honest with me. I love you, and I can forgive you if you're truthful."

Actually, I was bluffing. I had no idea if he had been unfaithful just one a single time, or if it had been happening regularly. Chester began to cry, grabbed my hand, said the infidelity was only once, and he had never seen the woman again. He begged me not to leave, and promised a million times that nothing like that would ever happen again.

I called his bluff, but had to be careful about what I wished for as I was not prepared to know the full truth. I prayed I was wrong, but I wasn't. In my heart, I knew it wasn't the first time, and wouldn't be the last. Sadly, in these instances, the wronged person becomes a bitch, because he or she is pissed off, and rightfully so. Then they become the bad guy and that becomes the other person's reason for cheating. I was a bitch because I intuitively knew something was wrong. Honestly, I was busy raising Dra, and I wasn't giving Chester all the attention he wanted. Is that a good excuse to be unfaithful?

Truthfully, I was feeling guilty myself, although I never had a full on affair. When it came to Luke, though, I was emotionally attached, as I had shared all of our marital problems with him before Draven was conceived. We were extremely attracted to each other from the moment we met, and it took everything we had not to go down that road. I was guilty, because when Luke kissed me that one time, well, let's just say I wanted to be with him.

Actually, I wanted to be with anyone other than my cheating husband. I was crushed, angry, and devastated, and being accused of being insecure pretty much pushed me over the edge. That's why renewing our wedding vows was like hitting the reset button. Let's give "us" another shot, because we did love each other more than we didn't.

Flying home from the VMA awards in New York with all the girlfriends from the band, knowing the truth from the horse's mouth, was torture. I really needed *my* people, and to be around my family and my friends. I yearned for my support system, but wondered if they all knew what had been going on and the joke was on me. Thank God for Vanessa, who was dating one of the Linkin Park band members, because she was my light in all the darkness. At least Draven and I could sit next to her on the plane. We were all pretty silent and tired from the awards show and all the hoopla that surrounded it. I was embarrassed and humiliated, but just having given birth to Draven, I was hopeful that we could work it out.

When we got home, pressure from recording the next album, upcoming tours, and a new baby, increased. Chester and I also decided to keep our friendships with Stacey, but to not work with her anymore. It turned out that we were great at being best friends but not great at working together. It was too hard to have one of my best friends as a nanny and personal assistant. This decision was best for all involved. It took space and time to get our friendship back and on track, but that was what was most important to all of us at the end of the day. Stacey knew everything that was going on in our lives, and saw it all first hand. She was so concerned for me and knew how heartbroken I was. She also knew what an extremely difficult time it was.

♥

I still wasn't feeling back to myself one hundred percent, so I decided to go to a doctor. Dr. Michael Cardenaz discovered that I needed a pretty intense surgery, more than what a tummy tuck would consist of, to reconnect my insides after my pregnancy. At the time, we had a new nanny who had a lot of issues. I thought she was sober and that we were all on the same page. I had even offered to pay her double-time for helping me around the clock with Draven while I healed from this latest surgery. We knew that I wouldn't be able to pick up Draven until I regained my strength.

The day of my surgery I wore my favorite bikini and told the doctor not to cut above the line of my bikini so I could always hide my scar. I thought this was pretty clever, but to my surprise, he said he had to make the incision higher and had no choice. He had to reconnect me from the very top of my rib cage to the very bottom of my pelvic bone. Holy crap! It would also take time for my skin to stretch back to where I could stand up straight and walk normally again.

My first day home from the hospital, the nanny, who had been with us for only a few months, decided to use drugs and almost overdosed in our home. I needed that kind of extra stress like I needed a hole in my head! She had guy problems and started to date a roadie for another band Chester was on tour with. That is where most of her problems came from. She was sad, hurt, and went to pills for her answers as to why this man wasn't going to settle down with her, or be what she needed or wanted.

I was just about to call 911, but her friends arrived (she apparently had called them before taking the pills) and got her to the hospital faster than an ambulance could. Next thing I knew I was on my own, right out of surgery, and on the phone with The Help Agency. I begged them to send me someone reliable right away. The situation was urgent because Chester was on tour and I was very concerned about taking care of Draven. Unfortunately, my mother-in-law couldn't get from Arizona to LA fast enough. She worked full time but dropped everything to come to us. I needed help right then, and I have to say, not being able to pick up my baby was the scariest feeling ever.

The good news is that is the day I met Girl Alex. Our family calls her that because I have a brother named Alex. We needed to be clear who we were speaking about. Alex at nineteen years of age came directly from the agency. That was what I called perfect, divine timing. As I invited Alex in and interviewed her, I thought she was lovely, a sweet young girl who came from great parents. She showed me her compassion and was amazing with Draven.

We wrapped up the interview, and as she was leaving, I told her she was hired. Alex was actually outside our front door and asked when she could start.

"How about right now?" I said.

Alex replied with a bouncy, "Okay," and in that moment I adopted her as a babysitter, assistant, and new member of our family. She was a lifesaver and I'm not exaggerating in the least. She saved two lives that day: Draven's and mine.

Alex told me she had major career goals and couldn't commit to more than one year with us. I respected her for that and understood. She was at the age where she needed to create her career, and being a nanny and personal assistant wasn't a long term gig. I wanted to raise my son, and any help I had was to back me up, not raise my child. That was my job.

I was quite impressed that this nineteen-year-old girl was brave enough to take on a job with a lot of responsibility. She also was not starstruck by Chester or his fame, which was exactly what I was looking for. We had so much fun on the road touring together, and everyone who met her seemed to adore her as much as I did.

When family members came to a show, they always wanted to spend time with Draven, so Girl Alex came to see the shows with me and hung out with all of us. It really was like having my baby sister with me.

Alex was with us for several months before she went on her first tour. She was very much adjusted to our lifestyle by that time and knew exactly how Chester and I liked to do things. After our last nanny I was apprehensive, but quickly found that Alex was the complete opposite, and that we could fully trust her in every way. I trusted her with my son, husband, money, and even with making decisions in the event she couldn't reach either one of us.

With her being so helpful, it gave our marriage a much needed breather while Chester and I tried to find our way back to each other. We were so stressed out before, with outside influences and a horrific nanny, that it had been draining on our marriage. Add to that the lack of sleep due to being new parents, and traveling more often than not.

Alex fit into our family perfectly. She and I created a healthy routine on the road and backed each other up. On our days off we took Draven to an aquarium or a zoo. If it was too cold we went to a mall, shopped, or grabbed lunch. Some days Chester joined us; other days he got much needed sleep. I loved our girl time and baby Dra time, when it was just the four of us or three of us hanging out on the bus. We'd be totally anti social and have PJ/movie days. Everyone needs some down time to re-group.

We also worked out every day on the bus when Draven napped, and our days off-tour and at home were some of the best days we had. Alex and I prayed to stay home. I know you wonder why we'd want to be home and not on tour with all these bands? Well, Chester and I had just bought our new dream home, and for the first year and a half we hardly got to enjoy it because we were on the road so much.

Alex and I discussed with Chester that we wanted some down time at home. I negotiated with him by begging for a week or two home, and then we would meet up with him. But, we were in agreement that, whenever he needed me, I would join the tour immediately. The thought of staying home made me so happy! Mostly, though, it was just a thought. As soon as Chester left, he'd surprise me with a call from his tour manager with our travel arrangements. Or, we'd wake up to a bus on our street, ready to load us up and take us back out. This was normally within two or three days of him leaving. Don't get me wrong, I wanted to be together but I also wanted to be at home. I tried to keep us in balance, especially as babies need routines, but I discovered that Draven adapted very easily to change.

The giant Prevost bus was our home away from home. The shower became our walk-in closet. Each of us had our own bunks that became dressers and sleepers, and the back of the bus became our master bedroom, instead of an additional lounge. The buses we rented when we parked, expanded, so we had extra space in the front lounge. That gave Draven more room to crawl, run, roll around, and do summersaults down the hallway.

I will never forget one night after Chester got off stage. Alex and I had gone to the bus with Dra, and as I was getting ready to put him in bed, a fan walked right on to our bus, scaring the shit out of us. I freaked out because I was in disbelief that a stranger would just walk through a family's front door!

When we got home we changed out our wardrobe, and had much needed quiet time without thousands of people around. It's the little things Alex and I came to appreciate the most. My favorite thing was to wake up (I was an early riser), make coffee, crank the music, and chill all day poolside. Getting that much-needed decompression and enjoying our beautiful, new home was a great way to spend our day.

Chester and I paved the way for the band when it came to having a wife on tour, and to marriage and family in general. We were already married when we met the guys from Linkin Park, so having other people who were not married try to impose rules on our marriage and tell us how many times we could see each other did not work for us. Actually, it was ridiculous. However, on the other hand, Chester and I were not clueless. We understood they were not married and that it was a lot to ask of others to be on the same bus with a married couple, especially a couple with a baby who woke up early and went to bed early. That was when we decided to get our own bus. Our own bus for our family was just what we needed, but it was an extra expense to us personally, until the rest of the band was in the same boat.

Touring is both life saving and life draining. It will build you up and destroy you all at the same time—without you realizing it. It is not nearly as glamorous as you think, and yet it's magical. Dreams are created, friendships are built, and babies are born.

After a two-year touring cycle with minimal time at home, I became resentful. I was such a foolish woman, because I believed with all my soul that my husband would not cheat on me, even if it was with Cindy Crawford or the entire squad of Dallas Cowboy Cheerleaders. I trusted him, but I was so, so wrong to do that. Eight months prior to actually serving Chester with divorce papers, I contacted an attorney. I just couldn't get past the adultery and was prepared to divorce him then. Our series of fights went like this: he messed up, got caught, I was pissed off and wouldn't let it go. Then he said I was being a bitch. Some of the arguments were also fueled by his on and off again over-use of drugs and alcohol. It all added up to a vicious and destructive cycle that we couldn't get out of.

When the band's manager found out about our upcoming divorce he called me and said, "Hun, it's the music biz. Turn the other cheek. You guys are madly in love with each other. He loves you more than anyone, and you have it all together. It's just sex, drugs, and rock 'n roll, babe. You know he loves you."

His heart was in the right place, I'm sure. Even my dad told me to turn the other cheek!

About this same time, our dog Tashi became very sick with cancer, and the vet suggested we put her down. I had Tashi before I met Chester, and was absolutely heartbroken over the news. We were standing in the kitchen and I was crying when he walked to me, pulled me into his arms and said, "Please call off the divorce. I love you." We both broke down and cried our hearts out. Chester later took Tashi to the vet and took care of her final moments. I was so grateful that he did that.

We continued to work on our marriage, finished the tour, and eight months later were working on his solo side project with several friends and artists whom Chester admired. I was so happy, because he had wanted to do this for some time. In January, Chester planned a trip to Indiana with his guy friends, but he and I were going to meet in Saint Louis, Missouri. I flew to Saint Louis with Draven, and Kim, our tour manager's assistant, met us there so she could help me with Dra. We were also meeting with Phil Sneed, guitarist/bassist for the band Story of the Year, and two other artists who might be involved in the side project. Phil lived in Saint Louis.

When I arrived, everything seemed normal. Then the day Chester was supposed to fly to us, he said he was snowed in. Yes, it was January, so snow was possible, but everyone else on that trip made it home to their wives and girlfriends. Why was Chester the only one snowed in? I was out with some of the crew for the rapper, Nelly. Two of the guys were close friends with us and also lived there in St. Louis. They offered to drive to pick Chester up, saying they could get through the snow with their trucks. I thought that was unbelievably kind of them, but Chester thought I was being a controlling wife. Interesting, to say the least.

I actually thought Chester wanted to be with his wife and son. I actually thought he wanted to do this side project. Finally, I broke down to Phil and his wife. Phil had become like a brother to me during touring. We had so much in common, especially being adopted from birth. I probably ruined our lovely afternoon by crying, and telling them this was the straw that broke the camel's back. Chester and I would be getting a divorce. They were the only people I told.

Chester finally showed up, and when I got back to the hotel and saw the condition my husband was in, it was a no brainer to get another room for Kim and Draven. I did not want them in harm's way of what was about to take place. I got the two of them situated in a suite, knowing I would be joining them as well, and contacted my attorney. "You know those papers we drew up several months ago?" I said. "Please have them ready when I land in LA. I will come right into the office and sign them."

I was still in love with Chester, and divorce was the last thing I wanted to do. But, I didn't like him at all and I had some self respect. That evening, as he was puking all over the place from his amazing, "guy's weekend," I said, "This is the last time I will put up with this. You can clean up your own puke. Oh, and I want a divorce."

Then I left Chester alone in that state, and went out with our friends who were waiting for us. We all continued with our plans that had previously been made, minus Chester. When I returned to the hotel after a long night out, the next morning is when it hit me. That's when the tears came rushing down and when reality sunk in. I still wasn't sure if I was doing the right thing, because we did love each other. We both wanted to be free of all the damage we had created, and the bottom line was that I loved myself and our son more than I loved Chester.

Once You Do it You Can Never Come Back

IT WAS JANUARY 14, 2004. I will never forget the date, because January 14 was my stepmonster's birthday. She apparently thought the entire world (or at least my world), revolved around her, which couldn't be farther from the truth! Can I just say: my nemesis.

As Chester, Draven, and I flew back to LA from Saint Louis, I realized this was the last time our family would be on a plane together. I remember taking that moment in so deeply. I made a mental note that I couldn't wait for a strong man to walk in and replace the shoes my husband once wore. One day, my son and I would travel like a normal family again, with a man who wanted to be in both of our lives. I'm just sharing that I wished for those things in that actual moment. I knew Chester loved us both and that this was a dark time for him, too. As I looked around at the other families on the plane, it hit me again how deeply important family is to me.

Never did I ever think this would happen to us. After I got home, I called Draven's godfather, Stef, with absolute devastation. Stef is the co-founder and lead guitarist for the metal band

Deftones, and is also my best male friend on the planet. I explained that it was done, the divorce papers were on their way to being served and signed. After a very public and tumultuous divorce—and when I say public, we were on television's *Celebrity Justice* right before the Michael Jackson trial—I was trying to survive the nasty tabloids, and raise my toddler son. Dealing with all the media, and all the extra "trash baggage," was completely unnecessary.

The tabloid site TMZ (Thirty-Mile Zone), also released information that was half true and half so far off base it was ridiculous. Whoever they paid for all the smut didn't do his or her homework. Or, most likely, they just made things up. Contrary to what fans or anyone else thinks, I divorced Chester, not the other way around. The files do not lie. The paperwork and legalities speak the truth.

I bought Chester out of our house to the penny, and we split everything else fifty-fifty. After the divorce I stayed in the music industry, owned my own record label, sang on house and dance music (that wasn't all that good!), and created a child meditation CD with a DJ friend, Kyle Hendrix, a.k.a. DJ Rain. I also became a life coach and an advance DNA Theta Healer, and co-produced several albums.

My silver lining was when Stef called me from tour. His landlord had a family emergency, and Stef now had thirty days to move out of his Manhattan Beach home, but he was on the road. This was not a silver lining for him, at least not at first. I also would never wish such a situation on Stef, or anyone else. It's tough to be uprooted from a home, and I knew this upcoming change brought him sadness. He loved his place at the beach, but we quickly thought of a plan. I always looked for those little silver linings, and this time I found one.

Stef didn't tell me about his situation for any reason other than sharing with me as a friend. "Don't worry," I said. "Let's get management or friends or whatever we need to do to get you moved while you are on tour. We can store all your furniture and belongings in my guest house, then figure everything else out when you get home."

When Stef got back we both thought it was a great idea for him to move in and take over the guest house. That would be a win-win situation. He needed a place to stay, and now as a single mom with a huge overhead, it was smart to rent out my guest home.

For the record, for all the crazies, gossipers, and rumor starters, Stef is, from the moment I met him, and always will be, my best friend. We have never dated, never hooked up. So sorry to disappoint everyone's incredibly bizarre imagination and distorted point of view. The guest house provided plenty of space for him, and when we traveled, one of us was always there to care for the animals and watch the houses. It was perfect, especially because we knew each other's friends. Stef also knew Chester very well, and that alone made everything much easier. I had hoped that peace would be restored in our home, and with Uncle Stef on-site, it most definitely had been. I felt a strong sense of safety and family now, and I'm sure he did, too.

Over the years of many barbecues, holidays, birthday parties with his famous cannon balls into the pool, showing off to the kiddos, and teaching them the "proper" way to make an entrance to the pool, Stef became the head male figure in our household. He and I also had many heart to heart discussions about life, and supported one another. I cannot thank him enough for being a pillar of strength through life's ebb and flow and for being one of the greatest male role model any child and friend could hope for. He means so much to both Draven and me. I just want to share with the entire world how important and what an amazing influence he has been in our lives, and continues to be.

Unconditional love is what I feel for Stef. I say this because I thought we could love only our children unconditionally. A mother's love for her child, or at least my love for my son, is unconditional. There's nothing he could do or not do to make me not love him or be there for him. In my marriages, or in any relationship or friendship for that matter, there are many conditions. If someone has hurt me or my son, cheated on me, stolen from me, or created lies or gossip, those are the conditions for me and my relationships. I can forgive, but that person will never be close to me or my family again. Rarely, we come across a "unicorn," and no matter what we go through, no matter what we say or do, the unicorn is there for us. Always. The unicorn is the exception to any rule. I love Stef unconditionally. He is family. He is also our unicorn and my exception.

At first, when Stef moved in, some friends and acquaintances became jealous, and didn't like that he was moving in. The only people it mattered to was Stef, Chester, Draven, and me. Chester knew that Stef had all of our best intentions at heart, including Chester's. Remember, Chester and I both choose him to be Draven's godfather. After the divorce, Chester and I had our differences at times, and discussed issues as a family or even fought about them, but deep down I knew Chester felt better knowing Draven's godpapa and "our" best friend was two hundred feet away.

Stef and I held the two forts down, and later, after the sting of our contentious divorce lessened, Chester and I found healing through co-parent counseling. We also found a stronger friendship as the years passed, but it didn't come easily. We fought to the point where I realized we spent far more time fighting with each other than I would have liked. I'm sure he felt the same.

Eventually, Chester and I got to a place where we could share our secrets of shame, share the true feelings each of us had, apologize, forgive, and make joint business and family decisions. Just about every subject you can think of, Chester and I discussed and ran by each other. Sometimes we discussed things as two parents should, because it was the right thing to do. Other times we shared things we had experienced, because no one else had as much history with each other as we did, and it was easier than explaining to anyone else. Chester also went to rehab several times after our divorce. I was pleased that he was trying to be more responsible and live a cleaner, more sober life, but he still struggled.

In 2010 I married my lovely friend from childhood, Tony Dominguez. Tony and I had been friends since we were twelve, but never dated as kids. We hung out when we were kids here and there, and sometimes at the random party we ran into each other hanging out with mutual friends back in the day, but he wasn't part of my daily life then. We ran into each other at a close mutual friend's funeral. With both of us being in the music industry (Tony is a sober coach for many actors, musicians, and other industry people) it was just a matter of time before we were meeting in New York, talking on the phone, and getting reacquainted. We also soon were jet setting between LA and NY, living at The Chateau Marmont, and at our Palos Verdes home. I loved our new worldly travels. After slowly building trust and building a friendship as adults, we began to date. When we fell in love, all seemed right in the world.

As time went on Tony and I realized we had opened each other's hearts to love again. That was our purpose together. Both of us were spiritual and practiced our beliefs. Walking the walk, we decided to go our separate ways. Maybe we were better off as friends? Maybe we rushed into things? The first person I called to discuss this with was Chester. After all, my decisions affected our son and him. He supported our choice without judgment. Tony and Chester both being sober and both knowing me so well got along better than I could have hoped for. Thank God!

I have had a very hard time with relationships since my divorce, and most likely I self-sabotaged my new marriage, instead of staying in it and fighting for it. But, there wasn't much to fight over. I was scared, but I don't know what I was scared of. Maybe I was just used to life being Draven and me. However, Tony is still one of the only men that I trust, and I do love him very much. I'm so sorry for hurting him and breaking our vows. I had said "yes" to for better or worse, and to loving him forever. It turned out I couldn't do all I promised, but there is a huge part of me that will always be in love with Tony.

As the years went by, and after my divorce from Tony, I understood that Stef and I would not be roommates forever. We lived harmoniously for about nine years, and were both ready to make some life changes that were better for us and our futures. Stef and his amazing girlfriend (I pray these two get married) finally moved in with each other, and eventually bought an amazing beach home.

Draven and I had been talking about moving for almost three years. He wanted to go to high school in a different area, because many of his closest friends were moving away. His best friend from pre-school had moved to Malibu, and his other closest friend, this one from kindergarten, had moved south to Encinitas. We had been house hunting for almost a year when Chester moved very close to our home in Palos Verdes. Honestly, after our divorce he had lived all over. He moved more than anyone I had ever known. On top of that he had to travel often, so he was always gone anyway. I didn't want to live that close to Chester. At least one city away would have been nice, right? We were still in co-parent counseling. Did he really want to grocery shop with me?

After we got through our issues, and I learned to move my own ego out of the way, both Chester and I agreed it was time for Draven and me to make a change. We deserved to be happy and I did offer to do all the commuting between parental visits. I kept Draven in a stable home for fifteen years, but we both wanted a change so badly. We also realized that Draven saw his father far more when we had planned visits, and much less when he was five minutes away. When Chester was that close, things came up and it was easy to cancel.

So, the house hunting resumed! With Chester's blessing, and that of our therapist, and I'm sure our attorneys, Draven and I searched up and down the coast. We did not want to leave California, but we looked all the way south from La Jolla Beach to north of Santa Barbara, a distance of some fifty or sixty miles. We also looked at every school in the areas we were serious about, and took every one of the long school tours. Moving south would have been a better move financially, but I grew up in the Pacific Palisades and Draven already had friends there, children of friends I grew up with. We kept in mind, too, that his friend from pre-school ended up in Malibu, just around the corner from the Palisades. That made our hearts light up!

We both wanted to move to a place where our souls lit up, and we also wanted a lifestyle change. We wanted a simple, easy life, and a major downsize in the size of our home so we could travel more. Draven was starting ninth grade, so high school experiences became more important to me for him than a huge house overflowing with toys. Our toys were big, but they were things such as surfboards, paddleboards, and golf carts. Draven would also have his own car soon. I didn't want to give up our amenities, but instead of having a giant backyard that needed major care and property taxes that were insane, we found a beautiful home with epic ocean views and all of our same amenities, with a smaller backyard. And, right across the street from our front door was a beautiful beach that has become our daily playground.

The beach and ocean have always been our "go to" place, but now we didn't have to find parking or lug anything. We also could walk to restaurants, shops, and grocery stores. I felt this provided our teenager with some new-found healthy freedom. Being between the ages of "too young" and "not old enough" can be difficult. I wanted a lifestyle change for our son as much as I was in need of change for myself.

When Chester and I first divorced I was fearful of getting that "phone call." You know, the one you get when a celebrity overdoses. I'm super spiritual so I always prayed, meditated, and cleared the negative energy for Chester, Draven, and me. Then came that moment when I wasn't afraid for Chester anymore. He was healthier than ever. His fitness was on point, and our conversation and clarity proved he was completely in the clear in every way.

Every Valentine's week Draven and I always took a trip somewhere. He was out of school for ski week, so we either did a tropical trip or a snow boarding trip. Chester knew that our son would always be my first Valentine, and that this was the one week a year we didn't share him. I admit I pulled the "I gave birth to him card" on this one. LMAO.

In 2015, the year Draven turned thirteen, we were in Park City, Utah with close friends. When I had recently met with him, I thought Chester was clean and sober, and the healthiest I had ever seen him. He was more independent and was spending more time with Draven on his own than he had in the past. Draven was very happy about doing things with his dad outside of his home, especially participating in parkour (an intense sport that involves climbing and jumping to buildings and obstacles without any assistive equipment), rock climbing, and when his dad joined our family and friends for birthday parties without his spouse or other kids. It made Draven feel like he didn't have to share, and he got his father's undivided attention.

Draven was snow boarding with friends when we all met up in the middle of the mountain. There, I received this bizarre text: I WON'T BE ABLE TO SEE DRAVEN FOR A COUPLE OF MONTHS, FYI. I looked at my phone in disbelief. Something was off.

"Mom, what's wrong?" Dra asked.

I showed him my phone and he shrugged. "Sounds like rehab," he said.

"No, Dra. Something's off, and yes it sounds like rehab, but I don't believe he needs that," I said.

No parent sends a text like that to another parent. I know Chester did, because I received it. That said, I think it was his way of telling me something was wrong, because that kind of text without explanation would set any parent off. I mean honestly, FYI, are you kidding me? So really, I was more worried than mad. Eventually, and I mean weeks after, I sent him a reply text. I had waited to send it because I wanted to trust Chester's words and give him some space. But, my eventual text read: LUCY, YOU HAVE SOME EXPLAINING TO DO! I was going for a Ricky Ricardo and Lucy kind of tone. I kept it light, but let him know that through my not knowing what was going on, I was running out of patience!

Chester replied with a screen shot of the number of days he'd been sober. He was in a rehab, again, but I still did not believe he needed to be there, because he had become so addicted to working out. He was in possibly the best physical shape of his life. I was sure that he was clean. You simply cannot be in that great of shape and be using substances. When he finally called, he asked if we could come visit and do a family weekend. "Yes," I said, "just tell us when." Unfortunately, the family weekend never happened.

Then Chester called. "As soon as I get home can I please take you and Draven out to dinner and explain everything?" he said.

"Of course," I replied. We decided on an early dinner and met at five P.M. at the California Pizza Kitchen in Torrance. When he started to share with us, I became increasingly concerned and empathized with his energy. I then asked the waiter for a glass of wine. I'm a "normie," someone who can drink and is not an alcoholic, slang for normal. In the past, I sometimes drank in front of Chester. He had been sober for years and had such a grip on his sobriety that it did not bother him. But, hearing what we were hearing from him, I needed to calm down.

I was upset with how much he shared with Draven and me. I even said that Draven was too young, and wondered if he should be included in the discussion. Chester was very angry that others put him in rehab without his true consent, and shared all his feelings with us both. These were very deep, personal feelings, concerns, and fears. It was so much to take in that my nerves became tight. I was very concerned for him and wondered how he was going to make some major, and needed, changes in his life. Change is always needed when we are unhappy, and Chester told us he was very unhappy—and angry.

As he continued to share, Draven and I glanced at each other to make sure we both had heard the same thing. Chester picked up on our concern, and I was convinced that everything was going to eventually be okay. I told him I would help any way I could. We had built a lifestyle together and I would always help him. If he needed a home, I would have said, "pick one." If he needed money, it was his. If he owed me money, we would work a payment plan. It was never the end. We both came from nothing and were self-made, so money didn't mean everything to us. Although, we did spend more money then most fighting our divorce. But since then we had come full circle and were back to being friends.

By the end of our dinner and conversation, with Draven and me doing most of the listening, I left feeling disturbed, but also feeling good that Chester had been so open and honest. Chester was so vulnerable, and my concerned shifted more to whether Draven could handle everything his dad had said.

Draven and I communicate well, so during the next few days I paid more attention to him, checked in with him, and asked more questions of him, all making sure he was emotionally sound. With our recent move to Malibu, with high school starting, and with so many other changes, such as a recent move, new school, making new friends, and navigating ninth grade, I knew it was time to check in with the co-parent therapist who Draven saw privately, and who Chester and I saw together. It was after one such session that Draven made the decision not to stay at his dad's anymore. He wanted to see his dad on his own terms. When a child turns fourteen in the state of California, he or she can then legally decide custodial parenting and visitation schedules, or at least a judge will take a child's choice into serious consideration.

I thought, holy shit, here we go into a huge battle! I was prepared for the worst, but after Chester expressed how unhappy he was with Draven's choice, he said calmly he didn't like the idea, but he understood. He wouldn't fight Draven on this. That was between the two of them. Draven was old enough where I didn't have to fight all his battles. It was important to me that father and son work on their relationship without me always involved. The time had come and my baby was growing up.

We closed on our new home in Malibu on August 10, 2016. At the tail end of February of 2017 I went to Phoenix to visit my old boss and friend, Doug, and his wife Patty. They owned a wellness center in Phoenix, and also one in Sedona. The Urban Wellness Center for Integrative Health is the name of the center, and it's amazing! It was the greatest wellness center I had ever seen, and had many moving, healing parts.

Moving is stressful, so I decided to make the trip a girls trip, with one of my best girlfriends, Cynthia. Cynthia was in the health and wellness business and was a partner in a company called LiveWell Industries in Newport Beach, California. Draven had just started school, and it was a long weekend, so he wanted to stay home. Everything worked out perfectly, as it should. And yes, we had family staying with Draven. I didn't, and wouldn't, leave him alone.

I am a life coach and certified, advanced DNA Theta Healer. With our history together, Doug and Patty thought I would be a good fit on their board of directors, and I thought it might be something Cynthia would be interested in as well. Why not make everything we do fun? After all, we are supposed to live! I was eager to be involved, although my motherhood and career kept me busy enough.

It was a miraculous trip on many levels. A girl's road trip! It was exactly what I needed after a huge move. The trip mixed in dear friends, a bit of business, a lot of spirituality, gorgeous scenery, shopping, tequila, a Jacuzzi, and amazing twinkle-lit outside dinners in the middle of the desert. I wish I could share every experience I've had. I've traveled the world and have had amazing experiences, but this trip was unlike any other. When I say miraculous, I do mean miraculous. For example, we were sitting in Doug and Patty's kitchen when Patty received a phone call from a Buddhist Christian nun, Ani Patty. Ani Patty works at the Christ Shambhala Monastery in the United Kingdom, directly with Buddha Maitreya, the Christ. Have you ever heard of Little Buddha? In the Buddhist religion it acknowledges that nothing is fixed or permanent, Change is always possible.

Over the phone, Ani Patty asked to speak to me. "I have a message from Buddha Maitreya that he would like to make an etheric weaver for Chester," she said. "He wondered if I could give it to him?" She further explained that Chester needed protection and the crystal in the dreamweaver, made by and with love directly from Buddha Maitreya himself, would help him.

It's not every day you receive a call like that. For years, people had tried to go through me to get to Chester. However, this was a message from a holy man, not a random fan. I had done divorce healings twice, one time for each time Chester and I got married. My intention was to disconnect the chords from each other. Spiritually, I believe when we are married we connect, and when we divorce, we should disconnect. Instead of our blended energy, disconnecting, by cutting energetic chords gives each person back their own energy.

I was reluctant both times, though, because my true nature as a healer means I believe in never being able to disconnect, because we are bound in "soul contracts." But, bound together through Draven, of course I would deliver the item.

I also was alarmed to hear that Buddha Maitreya had the notion that Chester was in need of protection, and my intuition felt the butterflies of fear. I then asked Ani Patty if Buddha Maitreya would make one for me as well. I figured it didn't hurt to ask, and he would do as his heart felt he should. When Ani Patti got back to me the next day, she said that Buddha Maitreya would make one for Chester and one for me. She asked what colors we liked and I told her I had a rainbow one currently. She instructed me to give my original dreamweaver, made by my dear friend Nicole, to Draven for his personal protection. Nicole is a very powerful angel, full of bright light, and she is an amazing healer that Draven and I worked with. We also became good friends through spiritual connections and healings, and the idea of her healings being passed to Draven was beautiful. When I called Draven, he chose cobalt blue for his dad. Blue was Draven's favorite color. When Draven was a baby, purple was his favorite color, and that was Chester's as well. Draven grew and blue became his favorite and he knew his dad now shared that in common with him.

♥

Over the next few months, Chester and Draven started to spend more time together in Malibu. Chester even started to get to know Draven's new friends. Overall, everything seemed pretty happy in our home as we settled in. One day we were on my upper deck, and Chester said we'd found a diamond of a home. He personally never wanted a huge home again, he said. Chester went on and on about the upkeep, and if anyone understood that, it was me.

"I couldn't agree more!" I said. A smaller home gave a feeling of being free, of not having so many people working around the home, and not having privacy.

A few weeks before Draven's fifteenth birthday the package arrived from Buddha Maitreya and Ani Patty. I opened it to find two boxes with rubber bands and sticky notes. One read, SAM, and the other, CHESTER. I never said anything to Chester; I was waiting until Dra and I gave it to him in person at Draven's family birthday dinner. The dinner was set for April 19th at seven P.M. at Kristy's in Malibu. Just our family and a few of Draven's friends would be there. It was a weeknight, so we kept it to a group of twenty-five or thirty people.

At this point in our relationship, Chester rarely took me by surprise. On Draven's birthday he showed up at our house at eleven in the morning. He said traffic was good and if it wasn't cool for him to stay in the house, he could wait in the car. "Of course traffic is good at this time of the morning," I said. "And don't be ridiculous. Why would you wait in your car until seven P.M.?" I looked at him as if he was nuts! Kind of laughing, I was busy running around for Draven's birthday. I told him to make himself at home. He could hang out, and that my adopted dad and brother Alex were arriving around three.

Chester hung out, handled business calls, and seemed totally relaxed. As the day progressed, he got on me often about being too trusting with people. He was right. But I argued back that I didn't want to live like that. I wanted to trust, to love, and have good people in my life. I did have amazing people in my life, but he was also right. I had a lot of "clingers" and needed to clean house. He got serious with me on many occasions about this, and he became somewhat of a buzz kill. He even slammed his hands down on my kitchen counter, and said with a raised voice, "Sam, you and I cannot trust anyone!" Over and over. It was starting to get on my nerves.

Just before my dad and brother arrived, there was a moment in our kitchen where I felt compelled to share the story about Buddha Maitreya. I handed Chester the crystal etheric weaver and explained it was a gift made directly from Buddha Maitreya himself. Chester lit up. He loved it! I showed him how to activate it to his own energy, clear negative energy, and infuse positive energy with light and love for his greatest and highest intentions from God/Source. From what I know, Chester kept it with him always, as was instructed.

As early evening approached more friends and family filtered in before meeting at the restaurant. We were all gathered around tables, and in the kitchen, telling stories and laughing up a storm. It felt like old times, and Draven and his friends were up and down the stairs from video games to grabbing snacks as they patiently waited for dinner. Everything felt right, but I remember feeling an energy shift. I felt I was empathing Chester's energy, just as I did when we went out to dinner at California Pizza Kitchen. I couldn't explain it, but I know I said something to Moni, Draven's godmother, and to Celine.

That night there were lots of stories and many laughs as our family celebrated with Draven and our friends. It was a fabulous night, with delicious food and incredible company, along with an amazing giant wave cake with a surfer on it, made by one of our Italian cousins. I shrugged off my odd feelings and enjoyed the celebration. It was the perfect birthday dinner, especially for a week night. Everyone had work or school the next day, but no one complained. We just enjoyed each other to the fullest as we took over the entire back area of Kristy's. It was our family thing.

As summer approached, we were still unpacking and downsizing, but becoming settled. Draven and I were looking forward to some staycation time in Malibu. Then the news of the suicide of Chris Cornell, lead singer for Soundgarden and Autoslave, hit, and I knew it affected Chester hard, as they were close friends. Chester was even godfather to Chris's kids. It was the same for me when Scott Weiland, lead vocalist from Stone Temple Pilots, passed away. Scott's passing broke my heart and rocked our household. It wasn't just my heartache for my friend, but for four more hearts: Scott and his wife, Mary, and their children, Noah, and Lucy. All I could think about was reaching Mary and the kids. No one would connect us by phone or email then, and even Chester kept us apart. It felt as if it was purposeful, but I knew Mary and I needed to be in contact with each other. I wanted to be there for her, and I knew she needed me to lean on. That's what true friends do, just jump in.

Chester was the godfather to Chris's kids, but I didn't know them. My friendship was with Scott and Mary, and their children, Noah, and Lucy. So much devastation, so much loss, so much sadness, far too young, too many left behind. In my eyes it was all so unnecessary. I cried many nights over the loss of Scott, and the loss Mary and the kids were going through. We both were blocked from each other for some unknown reason.

Several weeks after Chris passed, Chester called to say he just bought a new house and wanted Draven to come see it. I was shocked that he had bought a new house after our several discussions of not wanting a bigger home, and all the maintenance that came with it.

"Of course," I said, "Let me talk to Draven."

I told Draven that Dad had called, that he had just bought a new home and wanted him to visit for a week. That pissed off Draven, because he just went through standing up for himself and not wanting to go there for visits. Now, here we were, both parents asking him to go against his wishes. In a nutshell, Draven and I fought over this. I was bummed that my son was mad at me, but I demanded that he go because his dad was giving in to him, and he should at least visit.

Two days later I drove Draven to Chester's new house for a week-long visit, said hello, and gave Chester an envelope of documents of his that I had I found in the move: his GED, a copy of his passport, copies of his driver's license, etcetera. I put Draven's new dog, an adorable and stunning full breed Alaskan Husky named Apollo, in the car and waved goodbye to Draven and Chester. They waved backed and I drove home to Malibu.

Shortly after, I received a call from our dear friend Jay, who grew up with Chester and me, and who was our old roommate. Jay had always been there during the heaviest and worst of times, and still lived in Arizona. Now our sons were growing up together. Isn't that what all friendships hope for? To last long enough for all the kids to grow up and be friends? So cool! Jay mentioned he had some business in Burbank and was going to bring his son, Mason. He only had to work a night or two and wanted to make a little vacation out of it. They planned to come the next week. I would pick up Draven after his week at Chester's, and Jay and Mason would arrive that following Monday. I thought it was perfect, and we were so excited to have them in our new Malibu home.

I stayed with the boys one or two evenings when Jay had to work, and he stayed with them one night when it was my girlfriend Tara's birthday party in South Bay. Tara was a friend from middle school who was flying in from Vegas. I felt so blessed to have one of my closest guy friends visiting, the kids together, and a mini-reunion with some of my best girlfriends! What an amazing week.

I drove to South Bay to meet the girls, and we were having the greatest time. Chatty Cathy's all of us, lots of oysters, and too much wine. That combination meant I was way too tipsy. I called my friend Billy, a local boy I had known since high school, and asked if he could come get me, and if I could crash at his place until I felt better.

Then I called Jay, told him I wasn't feeling so hot, but would sleep it off and be home before the kids got up so we could make breakfast. Jay was then going to take them to Universal Studios.

When I got to Billy's I laid sideways on his bed, fully clothed, and passed out. At 2:08 A.M. I woke up, and popped straight up, gasping for air. Something was wrong. I knew I needed to get home to Draven. "Please go back to sleep," Billy said. "I can take you in an hour, then I will go in to work."

I was so upset. I demanded he take me to my car, or I was going to take a Lyft. He realized I was serious, got dressed and started to drive me back to the restaurant.

We had left Palos Verdes and were heading to the Redondo Beach/Hermosa area, where I left my car. On the way, we drove past the street that I would have turned right on to go to Chester's new house. But why would I go there? Chester was in Sedona and Draven was at home. I started to tell Billy how I fucking hated Palos Verdes and never wanted to come back. I had this disgust in my belly and again repeated I just had to get home to Malibu and Draven.

"Sam, settle down," he said. "I've never heard you talk like this."

He was right. I needed to get to my son, but didn't know why. My intuition was red flagging me all over the place, and I couldn't get home fast enough. I swear I drove home in less than thirty minutes. I flew down the streets and didn't care if I got pulled over. I needed to make sure Jay and the kids were okay. I didn't want to call, as they knew I was coming home before morning, and since I couldn't explain why I was so panicked, I didn't want to wake them and scare them over a feeling or a nightmare. I had already freaked poor Billy out.

When I walked upstairs, Jay and Mason were sleeping in Draven's room and Draven was in my bed. That was the only weird thing. When kids become teens, they never want to sleep in their parent's bed. I thought he'd be crashed on the couch with the TV on. But, the house was calm and the animals were sleeping, I looked at Draven and he reached out his hand to me. "Mom, I love you," he said.

"I love you too, baby, go back to bed. I'm going to take a shower and you need sleep for tomorrow. Sorry I woke you."

Everything was fine. My intuition was normally not wrong, but clearly this time it was.

Then Draven said again, "Mom, I love you, and I again said I loved him, too. I gave him a kiss on his forehead and went into my bathroom to get ready for bed. I got into my PJ's and thought how cute it was that my son had crashed in my room.

The next morning Jay and I both got up around seven. No matter what, I always woke up early, just like clockwork. We were downstairs having coffee, and I told him how the party was amazing, and how I woke up all freaked out, rushed home, and all was fine. So weird. By now the kids were up so they could get an early start for Universal Studios, and were in the living room watching TV. Jay and I were about to make breakfast when the phone rang.

What a lovely surprise, I thought. It was my girlfriend Shannon from the South Bay, and one of my Theta Healer sisters. "Sam?" she said.

I was all bubbly and wide awake, "Hi, honey," I said.

"Oh my God . . .," she paused. "You *don't* know?"

"Know what?" There was silence from Shannon's end. "Shannon?" I had to say her name several times. Then the pit in my belly came back.

"It's all over the news Sam. It's on TMZ. Oh my God, Chester's dead!"

I screamed, and then I dropped the phone.

Love Note

Dear Draven,

I wanted to write you this letter, even though I try to tell you and show you every day how much I love you, and how much you mean to me. It's very important to me that you will always have this letter to remind you of this, even when you grow older or if I'm not around.

The hardest day for me with you was being the bearer of the most horrific news of your father's passing. I'm so sorry, with all of my heart and soul. I delivered the news to you as gently and as privately as I possibly could.

I'm also sorry that we as parents couldn't keep our family together for you. None of this is your fault in any way. Your dad and I planned you, you were conceived from pure love from us both. I know you know everything happens for a reason, and that our divorce brought you your siblings.

I will always have a special place for your father in my heart, and I will always lead by example, to try to show you that within my actions. I loved your father very much, and after all, he gave me the greatest gift in the world by helping create you.

I am extremely proud of you in every way: the young man you have become, your dedication to your studies, your drive in absolutely everything you do, your passion and compassion for what you love and for others. You are incredibly articulate and are very selective in who you have in your inner circle. I learn from you everyday as well. I am your mother first, and a guide to you, but you are my best friend and favorite human being on the planet. I am so proud of how you remain so grounded and spiritual, and hope that stays with you throughout your lifetime.

As your mother, I hear regularly from people, daily, multiple times a day, what an amazing person you are. You are always welcome in people's homes, you're a pleasure to have around, and a very considerate young man. I will never get sick of hearing how many people love and respect you!

You cannot let your father's choices or mistakes define who you are as a man. I believe you can achieve anything you desire. I will always be in your corner, supporting you along your personal journey in life, and I know your father is now your guardian angel and is also helping guide you on your path.

I want to thank you for choosing both of us in heaven to be your parents. It is truly an honor to be your mother. And, there is no other human being I would rather go through this roller coaster of life with than you.

I love you with all the love imaginable and not imaginable. You make every day better, you are my sunshine, and everything and every choice I make is for your future and greatest, highest good with divine intentions.

I cannot wait to see how you enjoy your life's journey, and all the exciting adventures that come your way. Remember honey, this world is your playground. You are a strong and true survivor, and *we are here in this world to learn, grow, experience, and evolve in every way.*

Please enjoy your life every step of the way, and try to stay in your present moment as much as possible, along with being responsible and making the best choices possible. All that, in return, will make your life much easier.

I love you so very much!
Mom

A Year in the Woods

AFTER I DROPPED THE phone the morning of July 20, 2017, I went to Draven and Mason and said, "Please turn off any electronics, give me your phones, and I will explain as soon as I know more." I did not tell them what I had just heard. By this time, it was about nine-thirty. I looked at Jay and he new something was wrong, so I beckoned him upstairs to my bedroom. We shut the door and I told Jay about the phone call. He grabbed me and we both began to cry, but in disbelief, because no one from Chester's family, my business managers, or the band had called so we needed to verify it before I said anything to Draven.

I called Stef and my business manager right away. Both had heard, but neither had confirmation yet if it was true, or was just more tabloid false news. Thank God they were both so calm. Between going back and forth with them, and texting Chester's phone, Warner Bros. called, but I missed the call. I knew then in my gut that the news was true. I tried to call back but it was a secure Warner Bros. line, and didn't accept incoming calls. The phone rang again, and my business manager said the news was true. Then Stef called to say the same thing. Jay stayed with me as I broke down in tears, but I knew I had to tell Draven. He needed to hear it from me, and not from social media or anyplace else.

Fighting with Draven to visit his dad for a week, I realized, was absolutely worth the fight. I was so glad he went. I also realized that when I dropped Draven off on July 10th, the previous Monday, and gave Chester his personal papers, it was the last time I ever would see him. We said hello, he said thank you, we all smiled, we waved goodbye, and that was it. It was all so normal. The last time Draven ever saw his father was Friday morning, July 15, 2017.

Jay went down to ask Draven to meet me upstairs. Draven knew something was wrong and I sat him down and grabbed him tightly. Then I tried to tell him as calmly as possible the horrific news about his father. We both were gripping each other in hysteria and drowning in a waterfall of tears. There is no manual that explains how to tell your child that his father passed away. After we could catch our breaths, Jay and Mason joined us for support.

I was still in disbelief and texted Chester's cell phone at 11:09 that morning. I still have all of our texts. For this one, I typed, ARE YOU OKAY? Then I typed, YOU NEED TO TEXT ME BACK RIGHT THIS SECOND. I thought if he was alive and thought I was upset he would call me right back. I never heard from him. He was gone. Then I felt him, and our house became alive with electricity.

First my friend Karen and her daughter stopped by. Draven and her kids had attended pre-school together and had stayed friends. I couldn't see anyone just yet, though. I needed my family first. She understood; she just came as quickly as she could to support us. She was devastated, and I thank her for thinking of us.

Then my family, Draven's godparents, my cousin Sarah, and my brother David flew in. Friends and family arrived from all over the country. Some of my closest friends, and Girl Alex also arrived. I was overwhelmed, and even allowed my stepmonster in my home so she could be with her sons and husband. I was on an overdrive of emotion, and couldn't stop crying hysterically. Everyone just kept telling me to drink some wine, to try to calm down. We had so many family members in our home and we hadn't even had a house warming party yet. For some, this was the first time they had been to our new Malibu home, and it was under the worst of circumstances.

I also felt horrible for both Jay and Mason. Mason was just a teenager, like Draven. I wished I could have sheltered them both from this storm. Thank God Jay was so on top of it, because I was completely unraveled. I simply could not stop crying. Before I could even think about paparazzi we had tons of them coming directly to my front door. Somehow, they got through gates and lied to neighbors. Celine, Moni, and other family members kept pushing them away from my front door and gate, yelling at them to leave us alone. I felt badly for our poor neighbors, who didn't need the drama, but who were all so compassionate.

Everyone who stayed with us the entire day and into the evening (which was almost everyone), we catered dinner for, because it had been a long day and the kids especially needed to eat. Then we all decided to go to the beach. I grabbed a raw, ruby crystal that was about three inches wide and two inches thick, and we all went down to our private beach. Even Apollo came. It was high tide, so we stood on the little bridge with its cement staircase that leads to the sand and water. There, at the edge of the water, I said a prayer for Chester, with love from us all, and I kissed the ruby. The ruby was a symbol of Chester's heart, and we passed it around to each and everyone of us. The last one to touch the ruby was Draven. He cried and said, "I love you, Dad," before we kissed the ruby and threw it into the ocean.

All of us then went to Zuma Beach to ground ourselves in the sand, pray, listen to the waves, cry, run our feet through the water, and breathe in the fresh air. It felt good to be out of the house, safely surrounded by loved ones. Apollo was running up and down the beach when someone noticed that with every step he took his paws and steps were lighting up with plankton. Zuma Beach that night became a bioluminescent bay. I have only seen that happen twice before, once in the Mentawai Islands on a surf trip, and the other in Vieques Islands in Puerto Rico. This was special, and we all got to experience it together. For me personally, it felt as if Chester was there in spirit with us. Malibu is magical, in a positive Vortex, with the most angelic energy that vibes with humans. This was miraculous timing, and a very rare thing to occur. Let's just say that Malibu doesn't light up every year, and this was an incredible moment for us all. Especially for Draven and me; we honestly felt Chester was with us.

We had only lived in this home for eleven months when this horrific incident occurred. After, we didn't leave our home for four days. We simply couldn't. Media was always around, and honestly, we needed privacy. We were harassed regularly, to the point that Draven finally said, "Mom, we need to move temporarily." He pleaded with me to leave, and intuitively, I knew he was right.

Draven refused to go into the new Palos Verdes home his father had just purchased, and died in, no matter who was there, no matter who demanded he show up. No matter who blamed *me* for him not being there, he didn't want to go there when his dad was alive and he definitely did not want to go near the area without his father or me. He was so hell bent on that! We did meet Chester's mother and siblings for dinner to connect before the funeral. We hoped to find out what news we could, because we had not heard a single thing except whatever TMZ had stated publicly.

One casualty of our divorce was that Chester's mother said she didn't know how to reach us. I guess the distance of two states, Chester's and my remarriages, and several moves, caused her to lose touch. We exchanged info that evening. I was very happy to see my once mother-in-law. I still called her Mom, and it was great for Draven to see his grandma. Chester's dad, Lee, was not at the dinner.

We'd brought crystals that Draven hand-picked for each and every family member we saw at dinner that night. Nicole, my healer girlfriend, and I, supported Draven through this process. He wanted something special that spoke or reminded him of each family member. We got a crystal for everyone to keep, and a bunch of smaller rose quartz for each person to throw into the ocean. Draven wanted to go to the cliffs of Lunada Bay, so he could share the experience we had in Malibu with his siblings. But, traffic was horrible that evening, and it was getting late for his younger siblings. Draven's wish never happened. I'm sorry Draven, but we do not have control over each event that leads up to disappointment. Everyone grieves differently, and we were all exhausted.

Draven knew we tried our best with the greatest intentions, and each sibling does now have a very special crystal hand picked with love from him. Draven tried hard, and is as at peace with it as he can be. Before we all split up for the evening, Draven's little brother, who was maybe eleven, asked to speak with me privately. "Auntie Sam," he said, "why can't you bring Draven over? I really want him to come." He was sitting next to me, and like such a big boy he had asked to talk to me about this with such confidence.

"Honey, your brother is scared and made me promise I would not force him to go," I said. "I'm his mommy, and it's my job to protect him. If you told me you were scared and didn't want to do something, wouldn't you want me to protect you, too?" I think he understood, but it still didn't make his shattered, broken heart any happier, because it wasn't the answer he hoped for.

This was killing me beyond words. I had been close with that child since he was two months old. When he was a baby I took him everywhere with me, and watched him often because they all lived with us for one summer and into the winter. Yes, Draven's dad's new family lived in my home for a time. I even took his little brother on a Disney cruise to Mexico with Draven. I love this boy very much, and my heart was so devastated for all of our many losses.

It wasn't just the loss of Chester's life. It was much more than that. I love Chester's younger kids with all my being, and so does Draven. Time heals, and I prayed that after the shock of Chester's death wore off, all would settle one day and we could continue to be family. When I opened my home to my ex-husband and his new family, those actions spoke volumes. I have often been criticized for my actions, but until a person walks in my shoes, he or she cannot pass judgment

Chester was cremated, and his service was held on July 29, 2017. I had a lot of support from my side of the family. Grandma Jackie flew in, along with aunts, uncles, and all my closest cousins. My cousin Sarah even flew back in a second time to support us. All of those people, along with Moni, Chester's and my closest friends, and friends who helped his career along the way made our way to his funeral.

This was now the second hardest day of my life. I thought getting a divorce was one of the hardest days of my life, but I was wrong about that. That was easy, compared to telling our son that his daddy had passed away. Now, attending the funeral, it was the second hardest day I ever had to live through. In the middle of the funeral, Draven said, "Mom, I think I want to say something." That option had not been offered to him. I would have spoken up for him, as he had every right to say whatever he wanted, but he got nervous and changed his mind. I support my son with his decision. Period.

Through all this, Draven didn't leave my side. At one point he said, "He loved me over and over again." Right after he said that, he repeated himself several times, sometimes five or six times in a row. Each time I responded with, "I love you, too, honey." He needed reassurance that I loved him, that I was right there and wasn't leaving. I understood his fear and knew we both needed some major healing and a little bit of clarity before we made any major decisions.

Four days after the funeral we were on a flight to Bali. That was the soonest we could leave. I had to find flights, a hotel, connect with the right people, handle affairs at home, make sure our fur babies were cared for, and pack for a two-week spiritual journey. We knew we needed to pray and meditate, and we were going to meet a guru, Gede Sastra Kumala Putra, who was called "Papa Good-Day." This was thanks to my lovely South Bay ladies, who connected us with him. Draven and I also needed to give back and do some philanthropy while we were there. We took the red eye and I cried the entire time I was awake on the flight. The only time my tears stopped was when I finally cried myself to sleep. That has happened too many nights to count.

We stayed at the Ritz Carlton. I had never been there before, and having Draven there, I wanted us as comfortable as possible. I also wanted a high security hotel, as I needed to feel we were both safe. We also stayed in the village with our new family friend, Papa Gede. We worked with local orphans, visited villages, prayed under the seven waterfalls, and had private healings with the highest priest in dark crystal caves. We even met with an army major called Babinsa in Papa Gede's village, and Draven and I made the front page of the newspaper when we helped save sea turtles with Papa Gede, the military, and the police. That experience filled our hearts up with so much love. In times like these you look for positivity, light, and love anywhere you can find it.

During one of my own healings, I became very ill, and described everything to Papa Gede in detail. It felt like I was helping Chester go through a "spiritual carwash," something he had to navigate before he could move to a different dimension. It felt like my body was shutting down. Doctors were sent from the hotel and Papa Gede stayed by my side praying and continuing the healings.

"Samantha," he said. "Call your name into your heart. Your body needs to know it's you and not what you're experiencing." I did, in my mind, over and over. It took ten hours straight and I prayed to God with everything I had. I was so afraid I was going to die—and I couldn't leave Draven. There was no medical explanation for my illness, so I believe it was spiritual. Papa Gede said Chester was using my body to help himself cross over.

When we got home from Bali we came home to the overwhelming energy of Los Angeles. Draven and I had a very hard time grounding. We didn't want to be home, as there was zero peace or privacy as we tried to live through this tragedy. Then Mary Weiland called. I screamed with joy and started to cry. We now both shared the same experience in trying to reach each other through Chester and Scott's passing. We have since vowed that we will never change numbers or addresses again without giving them to each other. It wasn't on purpose from our end. We were busy and you never think something tragic is going to happen. I had also just moved and changed all my info. She had a previous move, too, but we picked back up right where we left off.

That week Draven and I met Mary and Lucy at the Loews Hotel in Santa Monica for dinner. In a bet, Chester had won a signed picture plaque of Scott Weiland when he was first starting out. In the divorce, Chester let me keep it since I had become closer to them over the years. It was hanging in my small entrance hallway in my master bedroom. "Let's give this to Noah and Lucy," I said to Draven. "It's their dad. It belongs to them."

As we left to meet them I took the picture off my wall, and after the long hugs and tears of greeting, Draven and I sat down and handed the plaque to Mary and Lucy. Noah was busy with a school thing, so couldn't make it that night. Mary argued with me at first. "Scott would have wanted you to keep this, Sam," she said.

"Maybe," I replied. "But the only things my son has from his father are items I have saved throughout our history together. Draven and I want Noah and Lucy to have everything they can of their father's."

In our hearts this was the right thing to do, and I got to enjoy the plaque and keep it safe all these years for them. We had a wonderful reunion.

Draven and I were grieving terribly and were still busy unpacking and settling into our new home. We hadn't had much time to enjoy it, and with so many intruders and paparazzi it was no longer our happy place. So, we decided to leave for Kauai to spend Christmas and the New Year holiday with family and friends.

This was an emotional trip. Beautiful but not perfect, and totally perfect all at the same time. When we arrived in Kauai, I finally felt I could breathe, but then I got the flu. I was down for the first five or six days. Uncle Scotty and his fiancée, Brooke, along with John Bavaro, (a friend I grew up with from South Bay) were the first to arrive—and they saved the day. While I was sick in bed they took Draven to the beach, kayaking, zip lining, and all over the island adventuring. We had all done these things before, but it was nice for them to have some quality time with Draven.

On Christmas Eve Mary, Noah, and Lucy arrived. On Christmas day my cousin Celine, Ernie, and their children, Michaella, Jojo, Luke, and Tony joined us, and right before the new year my cousin arrived! With Draven and me, that was a total of nineteen for the holidays. We rented a big home that fit us all. Let the healing continue.

The plan was, three days after we got back from Kauai, Draven and I would move to the east coast to get away from the paparazzi (and everyone else who was pulling at us) so we could privately grieve and figure out what our next move was. We also had to learn how to survive the new normal we had to live with. Removing ourselves was Draven's idea, and my son is a genius. I intuitively knew we needed solitude to grieve, privacy, and a fresh new prospective where no one knew who we were. We also needed a new experience so we would learn to grow through this tragedy that had turned our lives completely upside down.

When I said east coast, everyone assumed New York. I let them assume. It seemed safer, since there were some crazy people out there. With scary conspiracies and so many people in our lives we needed to be completely removed to see clearly and make the best decisions for our future and safety. Many friends asked, "What part of New York?" I always said, "Manhattan. The Upper East Side." No one expected anything less, so it worked out just fine.

We knew just four people in Charlottesville, Virginia, where we actually moved: a friend from South Bay and her three daughters. They are dear friends who experienced tragedy in their lives as well. I thought we could all lean on each other a bit. This was a temporary move for Draven and me. We'd be there a year maybe, or maybe Draven would finish high school there. While there, we took time to check out colleges, in the event Draven found a school he wanted to attend. He was torn about our great California colleges, but he loved the cold and snow, so we took advantage of our time.

As for me, I like to visit the snow on snowboarding trips, but I do not want to ever live in snow. I'm a beach bunny, raised on the California coast. When I lived in the Arizona desert for a few years with Chester, it was pure torture for me. I like to visit Arizona, but never in the summer. I needed the ocean to survive—or even a lake. I needed a body of water close by. My soul depended on it.

Charlottesville had a beach three hours away by car, and tons of vineyards. It was also a very artsy, musical, foodie kind of town. When it snowed, it was just a dusting, just enough to look magical with a hint of Christmas. Draven and I found a gorgeous, three story, eighty-three hundred square foot home on five acres of land that was modeled after one of the wealthiest towns in Italy, Villa D'este. There wasn't a lot of maintenance with this home, and the warmth of it was perfect. Draven and I fell in love with this extremely charming residence that we temporarily called home.

This, by far, was one of the scariest moves I had ever made, and I was completely out of my element. Not having family or many friends to lean on was difficult. Draven started to make friends at his new school, and me being the social butterfly that I am, we quickly built a support system. The people were so friendly in Charlottesville. It reminded me of a mix between Abbot Kinney (a street in Venice Beach, California with boutique shops and fun, organic foodie restaurants) meets New York—with a splash of Paris.

Another thing that was nice about where we choose to live is that we could jump on the train and in two hours be in Washington, DC. In three hours by train we were in New York City. This is where the adventure of healing, clarity, calm, and pushing through major fears was beginning to take place.

On our first night in our new home, a deer scratched at our window with its antlers. I was terrified. I had never lived in the woods before. Of course, I immediately started to decorate the house. I had to create a space that made Draven and me comfortable, and feel like it was our home.

Any time I left Charlottesville and traveled a little farther into Virginia, though, I got a little scared. I cannot stand racism! It is disgusting to me and I couldn't understand how it was 2018 and people were still so un-evolved. To see a Confederate flag flying high in people's front yards just freaked me the fuck out. Charlottesville was a melting pot with educated people, but take an hour's drive into the backwoods, and a person could be killed. Probably not, but it was scary all the same.

Hopefully I am being a little dramatic. Everyone I met asked if I was packing, meaning, did I own a gun?

Early on I became friends with a police officer named Zack, through a painter/friend, Chris. I was making new friends in the community, and thank God for my Australian girlfriend Fiona. She became a solid friend, one I could always count on, and was a life saver. Then I met a wonderful young lady, Megan, who became my assistant. She reminded me of Girl Alex, when she and I worked together. Megan quickly became family. Our Realtor®, Nikki, was a godsend, too. She was so fun and always helpful. My favorite local restaurant was Fardowners, and I loved my girl Nikki (a waitress there), as well as Teeter the bar tender, and Mark, the owner. I am so thankful they let Draven and me fly under the radar, grieve, and heal. They opened up their hearts and families to us, and I know we will be back to visit. I pinky swear!

We also met some Columbian neighbors, Paula and Simone. We loved them and their family, and they became our best friends in Charlottesville.

Twice, I flew back to California for business, and found our home extremely peaceful and in order. I felt comfortable going back for a two- or three-day trip. My family and friends were worried about our well being, and the very few that I could share space with and who could take time off work flew out to support us.

First was my cousin Sarah, and her daughter Sydney. They came in from Ohio. Then Jason flew in from Chicago. He stayed with Draven on one of my business trips, but also stayed so we had quality time, as well. My baby brother David (Uncle Davie) flew in from Peoria, Illinois where he lived at the time while opening a new Five Star Nutrition location. My sister, brother-in-law and nieces drove in from Michigan over Easter break. Cousin Sarah and Sydney were able to join us then. My friend Rob flew in from Hollywood for his birthday, and Cynthia came in from LA right after. Mark and his son

Anthony spent some great time with us, and I really leaned on Mark. While they were in town, we went into caves and did some major exploring. It was such a great time. Having family and friends come, even right up to the days before we moved home, gave us something to look forward to and was more healing for us than our guests could ever have realized.

As we got closer to the one-year anniversary of Chester's passing, I knew our family and friends couldn't always fly to us to make sure we were okay. I knew we needed to be surrounded by our loved ones and the majority of our family lived in California. Draven and I were ready to go back, and once we made that decision, we couldn't get home fast enough.

Draven's sixteen birthday was just around the corner on April 19th. We decided to spend his birthday in New York with his Aunt Tobi (Chester's sister), and her husband, Draven's Uncle John, and cousins Ben and Jacob. Upper East Side Manhattan, here we come! We settled into our hotel, and then had a big Italian dinner with the family. The next day we were to join my girl Toy and another girlfriend Nancy with her son Kevin. We all had a blast tearing up New York! We had met with an old acquaintance of mine and Chester's the night before, and he gave Draven one of his father's favorite guitars. Uncle John gave Draven his favorite guitar as well for his birthday. Those two gifts meant so much to Draven. I think it was the same feeling that Lucy had when she got the autographed photo and plaque of her dad's. The things is, these kids loved their fathers, and to have anything that made them feel closer or connected was special.

Grandma Susan, Chester's mom, also came for a short visit in our new East Coast home. That was the first time in years that we had quality time with her. It was just the three of us, and it was perfect. When she left we only had a week left, and my girlfriend Monika and her son Kody came for our last three days. We had an amazing visit at a local resort, Boar's Head, and spent time in the spring and poolside. The day after they left, the moving company arrived and we started to load all our things and ship cars back to California.

When we moved to Charlottesville we flew there with both Ferris and Willow, our Leopard and Snow Leopard Bengal cats, together in their carrier. Apollo is a service dog, and he flew with us, sitting at our feet. I travel so much and wanted Apollo to help with cancer patients and children, and his demeanor is amazing. I also now have anxiety, and he helps me get through the airports. I fly often for business and personal travel, and take Apollo when I can.

When we went to house hunt for the first time, we flew with Apollo to test the waters, as he was new with us, and it was his first flight. I have to say it was easier without all three animals, for sure. Apollo did fine both times, and as for Ferris and Willow, they did unbelievably well. It was more stress on Draven and me, making sure they were okay.

When we arrived in Charlottesville we ended up purchasing a new SUV. We needed a heavier vehicle with the snow and weather. But, now that we were moving back we were in a bit of a situation. We had a problem, but it was a great problem—kind of. When we moved to Malibu it took me six months to sell our house in Palos Verdes. Again, we were only in our Malibu home for eleven months when we fled. I did have rental property in Manhattan Beach that I purchased as an investment two years after my divorce in 2007. Since my early twenties, I always had rental property because I thought it best to have additional streams of revenue. When we moved East, I rented out our Malibu home for a year. Unfortunately—and fortunately—it took us less time to get everything settled in our minds and return home.

So, where would home be? Before we left, I listed our Manhattan Beach townhome and our Charlottesville home. Both sold in two weeks and closed one day apart from the other. I was truly blessed, but now we were homeless. With Malibu rented we didn't have a home to go to. I'd have to store our furniture and cars until we found another home. We decided to drive the SUV back and make it a road trip. Hopefully that would be a little easier on the pets—and us. Then we would have at least one vehicle while we were in LA.

Draven was not driving yet, because we wanted him to have a California license. But, I couldn't make the long, cross country drive alone. I called Mark for reinforcement and thank God he was able and willing. I did drive us from Charlottesville, Virginia to Nashville, Tennessee. It took a day and a half. We stayed at a hotel at night so the kitties and Apollo would not be so confined to one area.

Mark flew into Nashville and met us at the Loews Vanderbilt Plaza Hotel, which was super pet friendly and very nice. It gave us all a chance to relax. With Mark doing most of the driving, and me pitching in when he was tired, we were back home in California just in time for summer. It took us five nights from Nashville. I think I kissed the ground when we reached Malibu! Mark and his family were so incredible to Draven and me. We love them with every ounce of our being, and I am so glad Mark could bring us home.

We found a home in the Malibu hills that we had not seen personally. I tied it up in escrow so we would not lose it to another buyer—with a contingency that we could back out of the deal after seeing the home in person. You cannot rely on photos! However, there was hardly any inventory in Malibu. I figured it was great to roll the sales of our other two homes into an additional property. Then, we would always have an investment, and when Draven got older he would have a house of his own, or at least an investment. I was setting my son up for success in his future.

When we saw the home in person it was beautiful, but needed some work. My main reason for not purchasing it, though, was the very steep and winding canyon roads. I didn't want Draven, as a new driver, driving in and out of the canyon. This road through the canyon was not safe like Kanan-Dume Road was (the road through Kanan Canyon) and even that road can be dangerous.

I lined up a rental for us in Malibu, which cost more for one month in the summer than double the rent I was receiving on our place for a long term lease. The upside was we had our pets with us. With everything so uncertain in our lives, when we needed to leave Malibu, our home was rented before we even moved out. I never lost any income, and that was a blessing. All my son and I wanted was to be back in our home that we left due to lack of privacy and fear of the unknown. We had not left because that's what we wanted to do, we left because that's what we had do.

We met with our Realtor®, Bill Rhodes, who sold us our home in Malibu. We knew we were in great hands, as he knew exactly what we liked. He knew my business managers and how my team works, and he now is a part of my team. I love Bill! We looked all over Malibu, high and low. But, there was a bidding war on any property that was worth a damn and in a decent price range.

It was almost the one-year anniversary of Chester's passing, and our family planned to meet in Malibu, at Kristy's. I was putting a dinner together in honor of Chester so that Draven, Grandma Susan, and my immediate family (including Stef and Moni's families, and a few of our closest friends) had a healing moment to remember him with love.

For the anniversary, I had several dozen roses delivered to the restaurant, and placed Palo Santo sticks with Selenite stones on the tables for people to keep, use, burn, or throw into the ocean—whatever each person felt in their heart to do.

Palo Santo is important for use of smudging, like Native Americans do to clear out negative energies. Some use sage or white sage, but I like Palo Santo the best. Sage, to me, smells. Selenite is used for protection and clears out negative energy, and opens a clear path to your crown chakra so that higher, powerful vibrations can connect you closer to God/Source.

The plan was to revisit the beach after dinner and do exactly what we did the night he passed. I had a ruby stone to match the one we had thrown into the ocean one year ago. Our rental was up and we were still house hunting, so we checked into the Four Seasons for a week to have some R&R, and to get through the terribly hard week ahead. Chester's mother was flying in from Arizona and we still didn't have a home yet!

It was important to me that Grandma Susan and Draven were as comfortable as possible. I boarded our animals to give us some downtime, and to try to relax with all the sadness and grieving we had to push through. So many emotions. All I can say is, "Thank God for vino. Jesus juice to the rescue!"

We did get to relax poolside with our many friends and family who came each day to visit, hang, and just be supportive. I honestly couldn't have gotten through any of this without my ride or die ladies: Celine, Sarah, Moni, my business manager Stephanie; Mary; Helen, a friend from South Bay; Cynthia; Tara; my surfer friend Keala; Pamella; and Monika.

A year ago, I had collapsed on Helen butt naked in Barney's, trying to find a dress to wear to Chester's funeral. That is true friendship! Each of these women has been my rock through some serious times—and they still love me and like me. I thank them for knowing my heart and picking me up. Actually, saying I love them is a down right understatement.

It was July 20, 2018 and it had been one year since Chester left us, but it felt like one day. We gathered on the water on Zuma Beach, and I made a speech right from my heart. It definitely wasn't planned—as if I would be able to remember a planned speech anyway. We all threw the roses into the water, red and white. We kissed the ruby and Draven once again threw it into the ocean. We stayed as long as we could, and then everyone went home. Except for Draven and me. We went back to the Four Seasons.

Draven and I had never felt so displaced.

Love Note

Dear Chester,

It was love at first sight for us both. Everyone around us couldn't stand to be near us; they always yelled at us to go get a room. We had more passion in our pinky toes than most people had in their entire souls. Please know that I always believed in you, even during times you didn't believe in yourself. I never did anything intention- ally to hurt you; my intentions were always pure. We were young and had everything to gain and nothing to lose.

    We worked hard, and had a work ethic that most others don't possess. We also paved the way for your band in that we were the first to be married and first with a child. My dreams became yours and your dreams became mine—at least at first. You and I followed every dream we had, sacrificed our comfort, the way we lived, and ultimately, sacrificed our friendship and marriage. I truly thought we were a team and could make it through anything. I also trusted you through the majority of our marriage, and when we were apart, I missed you so much.

Even though we were together a little over ten years, for more than six out of our nine plus years of marriage I gave you my hard work and supported us both financially. I worked for a paycheck, so you could focus on your dream, which became our dream. You worked hard on your career and struggled, lived out of my car, and in and out of my family's homes. I gave you my inheritance, my home that was my investment for my future that I bought before we got married. In addition, I gave you my twenties and part of my thirties. I also gave birth to our beautiful son. You have no idea how grateful I am for that—even for the pain of childbirth! I worked until you didn't want me to, so we could focus on having Draven.

Inevitably, Draven and I experienced the drugs, the adultery, and the enormous loss of you. I couldn't beat you, and I wouldn't join you, so I set you free. When I served you divorce papers, I was hopeful that you would hit rock bottom and that maybe we could figure it out. Either way, I was going to give our son a happy household. Honestly, it was so bad for us both in the end that I was manifesting my home with my son without you.

During and after the divorce our son became my focus. I'm sorry if you felt abandoned. We grew apart, partly because I didn't like to do drugs. When you first received the divorce papers, eight months prior to the final serving, you stopped me from going through with it. I knew I had to get the papers served before the ten-year mark, because I didn't want you to owe me alimony for the rest of our lives. I didn't want us fighting over money forever. We got married with nothing, except the little investments I had accrued at the age of twenty-two. We built everything from absolutely nothing. Your job was as the drive through guy at Burger King, and I was in real estate. We lived paycheck to paycheck.

When you slandered me and claimed I stole all your money, that hurt me deeply because we both knew I didn't do any of that. You know I can prove that everything in our divorce was equal, and more than fair. We agreed on everything, remember? I guess it made it easier for you to say bad things about me. I get it, and appreciated you later explaining yourself and your actions. After living with you *not* as a married couple, I saw a clearer picture. I accepted your apologies and you accepted mine. We kept our friendship between you, Dra, and me quiet, so others would not interfere in it.

Later, we developed a beautiful friendship, and I thank you for that. We spent so much time together even after our divorce, and were in endless counseling and co-parent counseling. I was frustrated about that, and was upset about the jealousy and slander you put out when you were on a bender, or when we were fighting. I'm also grateful, and I knew you were as well, because through the fights and heartache we found ourselves healing.

Over time, we spoke about everything, even the uncomfortable stuff. I opened my home to your new family and allowed all of you to move in. You as my ex-husband, your new wife whom you had an affair with, your beautiful children, even the mother of your first child, your mother-in law, and the nanny.

I did this for the kids first, and for you secondly, to help you financially. That way you didn't have to pay your mortgage in Arizona *and* rent a place in California while you were attempting *in vitro*. We shared so many things with each other over the years, and we forgave each other. That is truly a blessing to me now.

At first, when we found out you were in rehab, Dra and I were concerned and afraid for you. I wanted to know where you were, because I intuitively felt you were sober. We knew in our hearts that you didn't belong there. We knew something was wrong. When you asked us to visit we were ready to be there anytime. Unfortunately, and fortunately, you kept us away from the chaos. For the most part, you always kept us safe.

When you asked us to dinner, I was nervous, as I didn't know what the hell was going on. But, when you told us how angry you were about being forced into rehab, I heard you loud and clear. I was upset with you when you shared how angry you were, and how you wanted a divorce from your current wife. I was very concerned about your deep, dark scary thoughts, and the fact that you could have come home in three months, but stayed for six because you didn't want to come home to your wife, or your life.

I was also upset because I thought that was way too much information for our son. He did not like being at your home in the first place and this news definitely didn't help matters. I thought, for God sakes he's only thirteen! Now I know I'm blessed, because our son and I heard everything together from your mouth to God's ears. After you passed away I was thankful you told Draven and me together. I didn't understand then, but I do now. Thank you. I know you were embarrassed, because you told me so several times. No need for that, we have been through hell and back together.

After you got out of rehab, I wished you would have taken the Palos Verdes house I was selling. At least that could have given you refuge to figure things out in a healthy manner. I also offered you the Malibu house to stay in with Draven. I could have stayed with a friend until you wrapped your head around things. I didn't know what else to do but offer you everything I had.

You started to spend so much time with us in Malibu. You showed up early, spent more time with Draven, and even with my dad and brothers. What's mine is yours, after all. We did it all together. Your God given talent, and our hard work, determination, ambition, an extreme amount of drive, and most of all, love, made it happen.

Chester, you were one of my soul mates and my best friend. Although we were not in love with each other in the end, I will always love you and hold a special place for you in my heart. You're the only man I had a child with, bought real estate with, and created an empire with. I have known you longer than I haven't known you.

Your words ring though my head and heart daily, and I remember what you said about not trusting anyone. I know you're right.

I wish I could have saved you. I'm not angry with you for telling Dra and me so much anymore, and I'm glad you're at peace. I can feel that you are. We were left in a shit storm and it's not been easy. I've had to protect our son from harm, and myself from harm, so I can be there for him. I've even had to defend our last name that we agreed I keep. The greed I have seen, and the darkness. I wish I could have sheltered our son from it all, but I was not successful. He saw and heard the truth from you, with his own eyes and ears first hand.

I do not care, or fear, what this letter may do. I can only speak from truth and love. I will not cower to those who feel they knew better or differently from our son and me. I will no longer live in fear as I try desperately to break the chain, since you took your own life. I do not seek false anything and there are many who know that these words are true. It's also not my job to convince anyone what we know or believe.

With you gone, our lives are forever turned upside down but we will always be within the light, holding a loving place for you in our hearts. I, we, will always love you, will always remember the good things. We will remember loving by choice. If they ever need anything I will share what I have with all of your children, and with our grand-babies. You always could, and still can, count on me.

Love,
Sam

The Best Version of Myself

WE HAD A FEW more days at the Four Seasons. While we stayed there we continued to house hunt. We ended up finding a home twenty to twenty-five minutes door-to-door to our Malibu home. It was perfect for us, and perfect for Apollo to run around safely in his own backyard. While our family was still in town we were able to take them on a walk-through of our new home.

We did still have to do inspections and walk-throughs, so until we closed and could move in, my wonderful cousin Carrie and her family took us in with all three animals. We wouldn't have made it without Carrie and Arran opening their home to us. I know we are a very hard group to take on. We had shuffled around for a year, and it was so taxing physically and emotionally for us both.

Through it all, I felt all the pressures of life, motherhood, providing, business, and the handling of our life that is public. While we stayed at the Four Seasons, we met another family who lived in the area, and they, too, had family visiting in town. These people were high spirited, and reminded me of our family when we were in a normal frame of mind. One night they asked if we wanted to join them for drinks, live music, and great company. Grandma Susan, Cynthia, and I all went. In all honesty, I was nervous because my nerves were shot, but I needed a healthy distraction now more than ever. Draven stayed at the hotel with cousins and friends, and we were right around the corner, less then five minutes away.

When we walked into the place, I fell in love with it instantly. The twinkle lights had my inner child and fairy-like ways vibrating on a higher frequency. Suddenly, a young women let out a squeal of excitement and disbelief. At first she scared the shit out of me, and sent me backward, stepping on Cynthia. But, she turned out to be one of the sweetest fans, and explained her excitement as she gave me a huge, warm hug. I'm sorry if I was shy with her. She caught me off guard and I hope she reads this so she knows how much I enjoyed meeting her.

When I got to the table I was shaken up because she caught me by surprise, but I tried not to let it show. I also prayed that our new friends wouldn't talk about what had been going on in our lives, and that we'd just have a conversation about things we liked in life instead. My prayers were answered. We had an amazing conversation, got to learn about each other's lives and careers, and it turned out to be a very normal night, under the most not normal of circumstances. It was what I needed. Sure, I like the finer things in life, but I also like normal, mellow things far more than pretentious events.

Everyone had something interesting to say. When Zack came and sat down next to me, we started to talk. We instantly had a connection and became great friends, and I became unbelievably stoked about having so much in common with someone who was not in the music business. Instead, Zack was a mixed martial arts (MMA) fighter. In that moment, I realized, I wasn't sad. Wait, that's not true. Yes, I was sad, but in that moment I felt free. Zack and I talked about surfing, traveling, and adventuring—all things in life that I love to do, or at least I used to before Chester passed. After Chester was gone, I was filled with the weight of the world on my shoulders in a way I had never experienced.

I was a mother who had been in fight or flight mode for a year, with hardly any joy and happiness. That combination was a disaster for a person like me, who is a firefly, and who loves life to the fullest, as I do. In a year of fear, sadness, confusion, and uncertainty, I was so far down the rabbit hole, I was drowning. I was only able to pull myself out and stay strong for Draven and my family. During this time, I had four or five emotional breakdowns and was staying in check with my mental health. These were the kind of breakdowns where I dropped to my knees and screamed and prayed to God with every ounce of my fucking soul!

Here, with Zack, I had met a friend who made me think of all the things I love about life, and most important, what I love about myself. While Zack and I talked, I didn't think about anything serious, or the many responsibilities that soon enough I would tackle one by one. When people meet me, they see a strong, extremely independent woman. People are used to seeing me in difficult scenarios and I'm better under pressure. "I've got this." "Sure, I can take care of the bill." "Yes, of course, that sucks but let's find the solution." It's easy for them to forget that I'm human and vulnerable.

I was having such a great time, but had to leave to get back to the hotel to greet more family. I honestly didn't want to leave these new friends. For a moment, I'd forgotten who I was to the world, and all of my pain. Instead, I remembered who I was as just me, a woman, and who my being was. After I left, Mom Susan and Cynthia stayed to enjoy the rest of the evening, and it made me happy to see them in a nice setting surrounded by good-natured people.

I was hopeful that I would see my new friend again. He was a complete stranger, someone I knew absolutely nothing about. But what we shared the night before, it was as if I had gotten a clean, fresh slate. Whoever could help me find happiness and my inner child, I wanted that person in my life forever and a day! It was such a rare thing to happen, and such a blessing from God. Thank you God/Source for putting someone in my path to remind me of my joy. This man reminded me to set my own soul free from other people's baggage, and that many choices in life were not mine, but affected me deeply.

The next day, bouncing back and forth from the family pool to the adult pool, Cynthia mentioned that a woman approached her after she saw my last name on a sign in the cabana by the pool. She asked which Bennington was here. Cynthia told her it was Samantha and family. It turned out the woman and I had known each other since 1999, briefly, through both of us working with Warner Bros. What a reunion this was! LA keeps everyone extremely busy, to say the least!

I did get to see my new friend Zack briefly, at the pool. I was bummed, because I was pulled in so many directions that I couldn't really hang out. A few days later Zack asked if I wanted to get together for a drink after his work. We met up and our conversation just flowed. We talked about fitness, I shared music with him, and we talked about my most favorite things ever: adventure and traveling.

The best part was, after that evening, we just started to hang out regularly, and it was very freeing for me. We went to the beach, changed into swimsuits in parking lots, swam in the waves, and watched the sunsets. We worked out together and, God knows after a year of moving, stress, and a lot of wine, I needed to get back to myself both emotionally and physically. I'm harder on myself than anyone else could be.

In my mind we were friends who had some type of soul contract, because I felt better around him every time we hung out. Thank God he was as adventurous as I was, because most people are not. Or others cannot make the time work, or cannot afford to just bounce out on a surf trip. This is when Zack and I started planning a trip to Bali together. I knew I needed to do a lot more healing on myself.

My son knew I needed to get away and breathe, too, just breathe. Draven encouraged me to travel with Zack because he knew I needed Bali. I needed an adult trip to just be me, not anything else. I was afraid of traveling in a third world country alone. With a man it was safer, or even with a girlfriend. Besides, it was more fun to have a travel partner. Although I do a lot of international travel alone, I was still fighting fear in general. I needed to get back to my spirituality.

Getting back to the best version of myself meant I could grow, and come back 100 percent better for both my son and me. So, I needed to dig deep and pull myself out of the rabbit hole. Draven is just as intuitive as I am, if not more. The difference between he and I is that I have more experience in life. But, as I teach him, his abilities have become stronger and much clearer.

It is so interesting that Zack seemed a lot older than he was. When we met I thought he was thirty-two, or maybe thirty-five. He was with his cousins, uncles, and family who were all around that age, so I assumed. And he had a beard, so that helped, lol. It was also in the way he carried himself. He had his shit together and was more mature then most men I knew no matter what age. It turned out we are a generation apart. But no matter, he became one of my best friends, and I hope that stays true until I die.

When I am around Zack, I get to be playful. If he said, "You want to go jump in the water at sunset even though it's freezing?" My response would be, "Okay, that sounds fun." With Zack, I'm not required to do all the thinking. With him, I give myself permission just to have fun and adventure. God could have put anyone in my life to help me get back to me. But I'm glad it was Zack, because he is awakening spiritually, and a good man with a beautiful soul. I see him!

♥

Draven and I closed once again on a new house on August 10, 2018. I changed all the flooring and had the entire inside of the house painted. I needed to be at the house every day for construction, so I left the animals with my cousin Carrie and checked into a nearby hotel. That way I could handle my daily business and Draven would be closer to his friends in Malibu for the end of summer.

We moved into our new home on August 15th and 16th. Having movers, furniture, boxes, and cars being delivered brought us back to chaos. But, three days later Zack and I were on a plane to Bali. I couldn't wait to see Guru Papa Good-Day Gede! Oh, how this trip was going to be fun. That's all I wanted. Of course I was pulling my soul out of the darkness and there would be one-on-one healings, but I knew that would happen no matter what. There was no way Papa Gede would let me come to Bali without he and I doing some deep aftermath clean-ups and tune-ups on my soul.

Our trip was amazing and filled with lots of adventuring, at least until Zack became extremely ill. Everyone experiences getting sick in Bali at least once. But, it scared me so much I jumped in to take care of him. I did not want to leave him alone for too long, even to call in doctors to get him antibiotics he desperately needed. Our adventure turned serious, and in all that quiet time and stillness we became closer friends, and shared a spiritual connection.

I have never had that kind of experience with the opposite sex before—and without the sex. Being intimate, and sharing our deepest darkest secrets with one another, helped pass the time while he recovered. Our bond was not sexual, but it became sacred on a level of pure, spiritual love vibration.

I healed many of my losses on this trip: Scott, Kirk, Chester, and Trey (Kirk's roommate). Kirk was one of the loves of my life. Talk about big shoes to fill, he was one of the closest men to me, not just as my friend, but as my lover, best friend, and companion. Our souls ran so deep. After my divorce from Chester, we dated, on and off, for seven and a half years, but we were free when we traveled. Kirk and I never had rules for each other, and we always came back together no matter where our worldly travels took us. I had a plane ticket to go see him, but a week before I was to go, he fell off the wagon and died from an overdose. Trey passed away a few years later. God knows how my heart felt so much loss and sadness; I was so fucking heartbroken. I was done with all this death!

To be near Zack made me happy, and I temporarily forgot my pain. I held on tightly to this amazing, unexpected friendship. Please instill your own friendships in your hearts, and don't ever forget. It is an honor for human beings to exchange energy, and it was an honor for Zack to be spontaneous, and choose to travel and share his time and energy with me. Hopefully he realizes it's an honor for him to receive my energy, friendship, and love in return. Every time we hug, I hope he feels an ounce, if not a trillion ounces, of love from me. That is the way he gives to me and how I feel in my soul. Thank you Zack, for allowing me to honestly share who I am with you, even if you don't fully understand all the time.

It's also an honor to me that each of you took time and energy to read my story. I spilled my heart onto these pages. Hopefully you will learn something. Hopefully you received a message or a tool to apply to your life that will help you, or heal whatever you need to heal.

Our adventures in Bali were taken from us too quickly, due to Zack's illness. But Draven and my family encouraged me to continue our adventure in hopes of being free and receiving continued healing. I needed joy, fun, and happiness. Zack's sickness reminded me of fear and death, and brought me a lot of sadness. I couldn't lose him, too.

It didn't help that it felt like Chester was with us every day. Back home, everywhere Draven and I went, houses and hotels lit up like Christmas. Lights flashed on and off, and chandeliers and lights became strobes lights. Draven and I were afraid at first, but we got used to it. Others around us, though, were often frightened. Draven and I learned to say, "Hi Dad," or "Hi Chester," and immediately, it all stopped. Once we acknowledged his presence he calmed down.

It's interesting that even from another dimension souls want to be acknowledged. Here in Bali, was Chester trying to tell me something? Warn me? In any event, Zack and I both pushed through. Zack pushed through feeling ill and I pushed through my fear of losing him. Next thing I knew we were off to Thailand.

Something didn't feel right in Thailand, but I was desperate to shake up that sick/death energy vibe. It was strong. I felt it, and had to dig deep within myself to get through the negative emotion that kept trying to suck me back down. Adventure, new experiences, change of scenery. All of those are healthy distractions, so I prayed, and remained hopeful that I would find what my soul was searching for. I also prayed that Zack would have his own life changing experiences that would serve him through his life journey.

The first thing we did in Thailand was visit the elephants. I'd wanted to take a private speed boat to the islands, and snorkel and play on the beaches. I had hoped the weather would be perfect, but our timing was a little late so we decided to see the elephants instead. We went to the Elephant Jungle Sanctuary through Ethical Elephant Adventures. The place was lovely, and had rescued several elephants. They nurtured, cared for, and loved them very much.

We were able to feed them, and it turned out that they love watermelons more than bananas. We played in the mud with them, which I didn't like as much as they did. They were really playful.

Then we got to bathe them and swim with them. One almost rolled over on me so I had to get out of the way, and fast! These are large, absolutely magical creatures, and I felt a lot of gratitude with this experience.

Then the weather shifted. That was not good news at all. A typhoon had hit the Philippines, and where we were, the weather was becoming drastic. There was not much we could do, and due to the very high winds, there was no way we could see the islands by boat. Zack and I had rooms at the Amatara Wellness Resort Phuket, which was absolutely stunning. We worked out, had some amazing fine dining, but still the weather grew worse. It was hard to find flights home, and some nights the resort wouldn't let us leave our room due to the extreme weather conditions. So, we watched movies and meditated.

Our friendship became much stronger, as I shared things with Zack that no one knew about, no one but God. I allowed myself to be vulnerable and soft. I cried a lot, and shared my deepest feelings. In doing so, I gave him an opportunity to get to know me and see my soul.

One thing I shared with Zack was that I missed Draven so much, as I had never been away from him for this long. With his godmother and aunts holding down everything at home, I wasn't worried about my son, but my soul needed and missed my baby. After all, he is my favorite person on the planet. I decided I had healed enough and it was time to go home and start the rebuilding process for us, our new life, and our new normal.

When Zack and I returned to Los Angeles I had the same feeling as when Draven and I returned from Bali. It was so hard to ground back into LA after emerging ourselves with the culture and so much spirituality in Bali. I wished we had stayed in Bali and hadn't gone to Thailand, but we tried, and nothing less than amazing experiences and growth came out of it.

Seeing Draven when I got home was the best thing ever! I hugged and hugged him, and smothered him with love. The best part was he had me back 100 percent. I came back exactly the way that we all hoped for, and was a lot more rested. I settled into finding myself, and much more healed, found peace and acceptance in how our lives were forever changed. Best of all, I had an undeniable knowing that my son and I were going to survive all of this.

After the jet lag wore off, I found balance within myself from the month-long journey. I dove into decorating and pulling our home together. In less than four months of owning our new home, I had made so many major changes to the house that Draven and I really started to love it. Of course we missed our Malibu house, and were eagerly waiting for our tenants' lease to expire so we could take back residency.

♥

Just when everything had started to feel normal, a tragic fire broke out in California on November 8, 2018. It would forever be known as the Woolsey Fire. I had an amazing meeting on that day, going over all of my businesses and felt back on track. An hour after my business manager and I wrapped up our long overdue powwow, she called to let me know our new home was under voluntary evacuation. She suggested we pack up and be ready, and of course we did just that.

I grew up in the Palisades Highlands so I knew to have the pet carriers and their food, water, and leashes ready. I packed the items from our safe, and Draven and I each packed a small bag with clothes and necessities. He packed cherished keepsakes from his dad's childhood, including Chester's stuffed animal walrus, and Draven's stuffed baby elephant, Tinsey. We did pack one painting of Chester that Danny Hill (a friend and former tour manager for the band POD) had made for Draven as a gift when his dad passed away. I even packed the cars with pillows and blankets, just in case we had to sleep in our cars. Two of our cars were parked facing down our driveway, in the event the fire department made the evacuation mandatory. Shortly after eleven that evening, Draven woke me up. "Mom," he said, "it's mandatory. We have to leave." Thank God my friend Paul was visiting. He drove Draven's SUV and I drove my BMW. We at least got two of our four cars out.

Draven has an SUV, but also recently received my father's old Benz. This vehicle had a long history with our family. Chester had bought it from my dad, and then gave it to his father, Lee. Grandpa Lee gifted it to Draven, and we just had it shipped from Arizona to Malibu. Currently, it was in the shop. The Porsche that Chester bought me as my "push present" for having Draven I had to leave behind. Draven can drive, but didn't have his license yet. Although, I would have let Draven drive my small BMW and follow Paul, while I drove the Porsche. There was a lot of sentimental value in the Porsche, and it would be Draven's one day anyway.

Draven didn't want me to drive due to all the smoke in the air. He was so afraid something would happen to me. "Honey, it's just a car, and it will stay here," I said. I did not like seeing him in fear of losing both his parents. I knew that's exactly what was going on in his mind.

We were so new to our area that I didn't know where to go. But, my instincts took me down to our house on the water. As we drove toward the beach I called around, trying to find a hotel room nearby. Everything was either booked or evacuated. I pulled into our local neighborhood store's parking lot to figure where we were going to stay, and was on the phone with the American Express travel department. We were exhausted and stuck, and both Paul and I needed to sleep before continuing on. We were hopeful that the fire department had put out the fires and we could go home in the morning, even though at this point it was approximately three AM. Thank God I packed those blankets and pillows!

At six AM a security guard knocked on my car window and said there was now a mandatory evacuation for all of Malibu! I called my tenants and told them to leave, and to grab their personal belongings. Paul and I gassed up both cars, let Apollo out, and I was back trying to find a place for all of us and the three animals. Everything was booked all the way past LAX, and we couldn't get to my family and friends in Santa Clarita, due to what was now multiple fires. Anyone in our family would have taken us in, but we couldn't get there because of so many road blocks, fire trucks, and police cars. It was like Armageddon!

Finally, we got a room at the Terranea Resort in Palos Verdes, near the area where we used to live. It was a pet friendly hotel, and was far enough away that we did not have to breathe in any of the smoke. The resort had one hundred eleven Malibu families staying there.

We kept the news on around the clock in the living room, so we could get information on both of our homes. As we watched the fires burn so close to our new home, and literally 360 degrees around our Malibu home, all we could do was pray and ask friends who were aerial fire fighters if our homes were still standing.

Clint was one such fire fighter—and a friend from Redondo Union High. Through my friend Monika, he gave us aerial updates on the fire.

Draven and I eventually took a walk with Apollo, and grabbed coffee at the little coffee shop within Terranea. Next door was a cute little clothing store, so we decided to go in to see if there was anything Draven and I needed, or could use, as we didn't have much with us. Draven was trying on some sweats when a woman and her husband started to talk to me about Apollo. They were very kind, and recognized Apollo from our walks on the beach in Malibu.

The woman was so sweet, and the conversation eventually turned toward energy and healing. We discovered that we were both into Theta Healing (healing through a deeper meditative state), and as a matter of fact, she knew the founder, Vianna Stibal. "I must introduce you some day," she said.

I was over the moon with the thought of that. We also discovered we lived across the street from each other and were neighbors. Then she said, "Please let me give you my number, so we can stay in touch." I handed her my phone and realized I had forgotten her name. I am so bad with names. So, I apologized and asked again for her name, and she said, "Alanis." She looked at me as if I should know who she was, but I didn't recognize her. "Alanis Morissette," she said.

I was floored, but not in the way she and her husband most likely expected—not as a fan, although I love her music. She was the catalyst of busting our previous business manager who embezzled millions of dollars from her, Linkin Park, and other artists. She brought justice to many, not just to herself or her family.

I was so happy I had the opportunity to thank her in person, and not just through business managers. That was an amazing moment, and I was honored to thank her personally from Draven and me—and Chester. Chester spoke so highly of her when he filled me in on the details of the sad saga that affected all of us. She looked at me as she put together how we knew each other, then she started to cry as she hugged me.

After, she grabbed Draven and started hugging and loving on him. It took everything I had not to join her in the water works, but I didn't want to break down in front of Draven. It was important for him to know that I was healing, and that he could once again count on my strength.

Alanis is a bright light and an angel who walks the Earth. I do hope one day to meet Vianna, and I'm so glad Alanis's home made it through the fires. Meeting her was such a miraculous moment, and gave confirmation on how the universe works, and how we are all connected in love. Draven adores her and asked me to play her music for him. After listening, he said, "Wow, Mom, she has a really incredible voice." His words were so authentic and beautiful.

When we were finally able to go back home we discovered that both our homes were in need of some construction and cleaning from the fires. We now have our Malibu home back and are getting ready to move back in, while the other home is receiving some roof repair. Here we go again, but I'm happy about the shuffling around this time, and so is Draven. We now have our "family home" and our "beach home." We recognize our blessings and live in extreme gratitude.

Recently, I vowed to myself and Draven that we will no longer live unhappily. This year, we decided to honor Chester and Chester's family, along with many friends in Arizona, for Chester's birthday. Thanks to Raul "Ice Man," owner of Sonoran Ice Creations, for creating an ice sculpture of Chester singing to his fans. Raul also released forty-three doves for Chester's forty-third birthday. Raul's friend Jacob, from the band Lethal Injection, helped organize the venue Club Red in Mesa, Arizona, and helped me organize several bands that played in honor of his life.

This was Draven's wish, and Grandpa Lee, Grandma Susan, and Aunt Tobi, along with many friends and fans joined us for this celebration of life. We hope it gave everyone healthy healing and much-needed closure.

My son and I are not going to grieve in extreme pain anymore. We will always miss and love Chester with all of our hearts. I will always honor him and share loving and funny stories with Draven. I want my son to live a normal life. He has that right, and should be happy. He has so much to look forward to, and I want him to embrace life, and not feel guilty about being happy.

Draven deserves to have girlfriends, go to parties, experience college, travel the world, get married, and have children of his own. I want all these things for him; he truly deserves all the happiness in the world. And, I deserve happiness as well. I want to live, be free, allow my inner child to fully play, fall in love, and live the rest of my life in the happiest ways I can. We are on this planet to learn and to love. I give ourselves full permission to live life to the fullest, and know that Chester would want this for us as well.

−THE END−

Acknowledgements

I WOULD LIKE TO express my deepest and humblest gratitude to God, the Universe, and the Divine Spirit of Love, who has given me the strength, courage, and the opportunity to share my life journey with the world. It is truly an honor to create and share my energy, and exchange energy with all of you.

Special thanks to Lisa Wysocky, my incredible editor. Thank you for seeing my vision, hearing my voice, and maintaining and capturing my true essence. She has believed in me from the very beginning and kept my book in the high vibration and within the integrity this project deserves. I cannot express enough how truly grateful I am that she remains in the light with me on my ultimate vision.

I am beyond grateful to Stephanie Green, my business manager and family trusted friend. She is my mentor, and on many occasions my left and right hand. I honestly feel she is an angel, and that God has blessed my son and me with her in our lives. We both know that she always has our best interests at heart. I love her for so many reasons but mainly for just being the amazing human she is.

With all my heart, I thank the most precious person in the world to me. My amazing and talented son, Draven for all his love and support in this journey called "life," and for taking the challenge and having full creative control on the art and cover for my book. His decision to participate made the book that much more special, in every way, not just for me as his mother, but also for all the readers. It is such a beautiful opportunity to co-create with my son.

Love and thanks to Todd Gallopo and the entire team at Meat and Potatoes for the creation of my brand identity, and to Pamella Jean for her brilliant strategic marketing, and for sticking by my side through the radical and magical music industry.

With my whole heart, a special thanks to Ryan Greene for not only being one of my best friends, but for knowing me so well and pushing me to be the best I can be always. His talent, friendship, and love always keeps me inspired, and I thank him for creating my audio book, and helping make my dreams come true.

A special shout out to Neville Johnson, Daniel Lifschitz, Jay Cooper, Todd Cooper, Kenneth Bury, and Michael Elson for guiding me along my literary, music, and business adventure throughout the years, as well as this special book project that has been years in the making. Each has provided me with guidance, protection, and wisdom. I have learned so much from each of them, and I'm grateful that they are my "Legal Dream Team."

Tons of love to my family. I couldn't have survived without each and every one. Love to Jackie Kallen for loving me, accepting me, and always being there as a mother would. Thanks, too, to Brad, Brian, and the entire Kallen family.

Thank you to David and Alex Olit for being the best baby brothers ever, and to Scott Stephan for being the best big brother a girl could ever hand pick. Christina Taite is the perfect sister, and I love our very special bond, along with my brother in law Craig Taite, and my beautiful nieces Adrianna and Gianna Taite.

Love to Celine Ciacco (my ride or die) and Ernie Ciaccio (and the entire Ciaccio tribe of seven, including Christian, Michaella, Jordan, Luke, and Tony). To Sarah and Sydney Myers, thank you for all your love and continuous support. No matter how far away we are, we always find a way to be together.

Marsha and Todd Adamson, you hands down are the coolest aunt and uncle. You both taught me so much throughout the years. So did my cousins Falon (and her son Maddox), and Ethan and Stevie, and their son Griffin. Thank you Carrie and Arran Treadway and their sons Cal and Tyler for being my a.k.a. a little sister and for opening your home to us; Ava Rose for teaching us all to unconditionally love.

Thanks to Amy Brownstein for amazing public relations. Thanks also to Laura Ackerman and Karson Bankhead for their amazing public relations, along with special thanks to Jeremy Tick for distribution and branding, Whitney Marston Pierce for website design, and Laura Vogel for social media. Our team is brilliant and forward-thinking, extremely creative, and thinks out-of-the-box. I appreciate you all and thank you for joining me on this journey. Thank you for being a part of our team!

Thank you Chester for sharing the many gifts we proudly created together. Lee Bennington ("Pops") and Susan Eubanks, you both have always treated me as if I was your own daughter. Thank you Tobi, John, and my two nephews, Jacob and Ben Knehr, for being pillars of strength and the greatest sister and brother in law. Rene Brugman and family: thank you for answering the phone that day and for being my sister.

Thanks also to Stephan Carpenter for being my best friend and the best godfather any kid could ever hope for. To Monica Vasquez: thank you for being my best friend and hands down the most amazing godmother. I am so thankful for two very present and hands on godparents.

I also want to thank many of my friends, including Karen Hartov and family, Natalie Moddeb, Damon and Lili Geller and family, Stacey Cabrera and family; Helen Crutchfield-Christoni and family; Leisha Apker-Horin and family; Alexis O'Neal-Paterson and family, Meagan O'Neil and family, Mark and Sal Dicarlo, Jason Pastiak, Jay and Mason Kereny, Mary Weiland and family, Kelly Shaddix and family. Tamar Glazer and family, Joniann Taylor and family, Cece Woods, Zack Kraschinsky, David Boyko, Dave and Stacey Buckner and family, Katy Ferrel and family; Monika Manson; Michelle Zac, Erica and Dirk Vermin; Diva Borrelli; Kealla Kennely (KK), David Resnik, Danny Hill and his beautiful girls Jordan and Anna, Kirk and Reme McNulty, Jeff Blue, Shannon Lewis, Theresa Gage, Reid Esterson, Megan Morris, Alex Heller, Kristin Ritella, Sarah Killian, Ani Patty, Buddah Maitreya, Doug and Patty Edgelow, Billy Woods, and Kelly McGearyn. Thank you all for your love, support, and believing in me in this very personal project, for growing up with me, the laughter and the tears, the good times and the not so good times. We have all been through a lot and I'm in deepest gratitude to you all! This is what friendships are for, and I couldn't have finished this without each of you! If I have omitted anyone, know that it was unintentional. You know who you are, and I thank you.

Samantha Bennington grew up in Southern California, and was married to Chester Bennington, lead singer of Linkin Park from 1996-2005. She now lives with her son, Draven Bennington, in California, and is a certified life coach, certified advanced DNA theta healer, author, blogger; and music consultant and producer. Find her online at samanthabennington.com.